Editors

Travis Denton & Katie Chaple

International Editor

Thomas Lux

Layout & Design

Travis Denton

Special Thanks to

Poetry@TECH,
the Department of Literature, Media and Communication
and Georgia Tech's Ivan Allen College

terminus is published with generous support from

Poetry@TECH
www.poetry.gatech.edu

terminus seeks to publish the most thought-provoking, socially and culturally aware writing available. While we want to push the boundaries of general aesthetics and standards, we also want to publish writing that is accessible to a wide audience. We seek to live up to the highest standards in publishing, always growing and reaching new levels of understanding and awareness both within our immediate community and within the greater communities of our country and world. *terminus* accepts unsolicited submissions year-round, but keep in mind that most of our content is solicited. We encourage simultaneous submissions, so long as we are notified. Address all correspondence to: ***terminusmagazine@gmail.com***.

terminus is printed by Lightning Source and distributed by Ingram.

ISBN: 978-1-936196-89-0

The *terminus* logo was designed by Natalie Farr

Front & Back Covers, inside covers, insert and all things artsy
by Atlanta artist Charles Keiger
Front Cover: *Tulips (Homecoming)*. 18x16, Oil on Panel. 2012.
Inside Cover: *Inside the Bird Museum*. 22x24, Oil on Wood. 2013.
Back Cover: *Tidal Audit*. 28x25, Oil on Canvas. 2010.
Back Inside Cover: *Conjure*. 16x18. Oil on Wood. 2013.
Learn more about Charles Keiger's work on his blog:

http://charleskeiger.blogspot.com/

Contents

Featuring
Poetry@TECH's 2013-14 Visiting Poets

Art

Poetry

NonFiction

Fiction

Georgia Tech's
School of Literature,
Media,
and Communication presents

Georgia Tech | **Ivan Allen College** of Liberal Arts

www.poetry.gatech.edu

poetry
at Tech

bruce mcever presents
an evening of poetry   featuring

February 6, 2014
location
Kress Auditorium   7:30 p.m.

sandra meek

Thomas Lux,   the Marga ret T. and Henry C. Bou rne J r.
chair in poetry, introduces the Twelfth Annual

bourne poetry
reading featuring

September 26, 2013
location
Kress Auditorium   7:30 p.m.

bruce mcever

rupert fike

terrance hayes

afaa michael weaver

an evening with
international poets   featuring

March 14, 2014
location
soon to be announced

klaus martens

micheal o'siadhail

adam stephens night out
for poetry featuring

November 7, 2013
location
7:30 p.m.   Kress Auditorium

anne marie macari

stephen dunn

africa / atlanta project
reading featuring

April 3, 2014
location
Kress Auditorium   7:30 p.m.

cornelius eady

2014 McEver   Visiting Chair Poets

Ginger Mu rchison   David Bottoms   Travis Wayne Denton

2014 McEver   Visiting Chairs in Community Outreach

Katie Chaple   Theresa Davis

patricia smith

kurtis lamkin

THE KRESS AUDITORIUM
Institute of Paper Science &
Technology at Georgia Tech
500 Tenth Street, NW
Atlanta, GA 30309

All events are free and open to the public.
No tickets or reservations are required.
A book sale and signing to follow all readings.

The Kress Auditorium Parking:
Plenty of free parking available just in front
of the building's entrance or through the
gate, which is straight ahead as you turn off
10th Street.
for more directions & parking info visit:
www.ipst.gatech.edu/amp/

for more information about
Free Poetry Workshops in
the community go to
www.poetry.gatech.edu/poetry_class.html

Kurt Brown

Plum Blossoms

I am not going to read another poem that refers to plum blossoms.
Not after all these centuries, all that wind and weather
scattering them across the lines of countless poets from Li Po to
    John Ashbery.
I have never even *seen* a plum blossom, not in my entire life,
and I am over the hill now, or at least standing squarely on top of it,
and there are no plum trees much less blossoming plum trees in sight.
I am beginning to doubt the veracity of plum blossoms.
My tomato plant has just begun to blossom, so I can testify to that,
to the tiny yellow five-petaled stars that give way, eventually,
to hard green globes of fruit that will swell into big juicy orbs later this
    summer.
Tomato blossoms are American. They are real. Plum blossoms
exist only in haikus from the far east and haikus themselves
are like tiny blossoms, little syllabic flowers that bloom into the void
and keep on blooming, if they're written right, until they are as big as the
    cosmos,
which is a kind of tree on which the thoughts of poets blossom,
shedding light forever down through the centuries whether we believe in
    them or not.

A Photograph of Charles Simic

He's smiling at himself smiling out at you,
a wide ironic grin stretching from ear to ear.
His shoulders are slightly hunched inward
the way we do when we chuckle, a kind
of self-hug at the joy of simply getting the joke.
There's a merriment in his eyes that says:
I love this life, even if I will never know
what it means, even if it means nothing,
which is what he suspects, I suspect, though
he can't quite conceal his joy in living it.

Pan Del Muerto

In Mexico, they bake bread
for those who died—flat
little cakes they leave around the house
for a mother or father or a child
to find. The dead are living
like us, growing fat, paying their debts,
brushing their teeth on schedule.
Sometimes it's hard to make your way
across a room to shake someone's
hand or give them a drink. The dead
are always there, in their evening gowns
and tuxedoes, expecting to be served—
asking for more crackers or champagne.
Just making love is a sacrilege!
The grandmother is there and the school
teacher and the delicate sister,
even those who are not yet born,
more innocent than babies. You get
up in the morning to comb your
hair and you are combing the brittle hair
of the dead, which goes on growing
like the eyelids and the finger
nails, as if the body were the last
to know or simply stubborn.
And maybe that's what the cakes are for—
to nourish the vanity of the corpse,
who after all would like to look
as good as possible on such a great
occasion. Listen! You hear the leaves

cracking faintly at dusk, a tire humming
on dry pavement, the sound of water
rushing through a pipe? The dead
are hungry! You must take
your knives and bowls and go down
into the cellar; you must begin to chant
those old recipes you've been saving—
mixing your own blood with the dry
sand the dead grow fat on,
that the children of the dead roll
into loaves for you to eat—
for the dust that will eventually pass
entirely through you.

Riding Out the Light

Have you noticed lately
so many old men shuffling
down the sidewalk, taking baby steps
as if their backs were broken,
as if they were tip-toeing home
too late for their own good, trying hard
not to unbalance the set-upon
domestic order of things.

And have you noticed how they place
each sole gingerly down,
or simply drag themselves along
like obstinate boys,
like cattle driven into a blind canyon
from which even they can see
with their laboring brains
there is no escape.

On every corner, old men.
Mincing home in shabby coats—
maybe they're heading out:
a Grand Parade of Patriarchs
just now turning the corner;
gray procession in the evening light,
pale hair catching a last
glint of sun as it disappears.

Poemscape

Look, I don't mind telling you: this is probably—what?—the fiftieth revision
        of a poem
I've been trying to write for years and there's no guarantee I'll get it down now,
        only
I can't seem to give it up because it involves something personal, but also
        universal,
and that's grounds for any real poem to exist, a kind of literary birthright,
        or at least
a sign it's worthwhile to keep slogging away in case the Muse finally favors me with a smile.

    *

The thing is: it could be any poem I've been trying to write—and there are many—
        scads of false starts
and dithering ends where I'm trying to wind up with a bang, resounding chords
        of a concert,
a smash hit over left field wall, boundless effort put into an upshot, as if the middle
        were a bridge
and all that mattered was crossing it to get to the fabulous city on the other side,
        legendary capital
of an empire everyone suspects doesn't really exist except in the province of Imagination.

    *

The "Muse," the "province of Imagination"... What am I saying? So much claptrap
        from mythology,
this struggle to connect myself to something I really don't understand
        and never did,
though it may be the "Muse" is nothing more than Imagination itself and that city
        is my brain—
Byzantium of gray matter, kingdom of cortex and cerebellum—though I'm waffling
        now,

uncertain if my daydreams are the destination or an island where cannibals eat you up.

*

Let's not forget the poem I'm trying to write: it could be about anything, in any form,
        that's not the point,
and the language is mixed, whatever works at the time, whatever doesn't get in the way
        of what's being said,
something I really care about personally, though we all know what happened
        to sincerity
once the critics got ahold of it, and there is no "I" to care about anything, much less
        the poem I'm writing,
which you will interpret in any way you see fit so why bother to angle at a single goal.

*

Is this *really* the draft of a poem, or am I shadow-boxing, wasting your time and mine,
        though you've guessed by now
that what I'm doing is a ploy to write a poem avoiding what I started out to write—
        that proto-poem
I've dragged through many stages, many scarred attempts—so this is actually a meta-
  poem,
        as if my mind
and how it works were more engrossing and "sincere" than anything I might intend,
        the "real" poem so to speak,
not some dumb contrivance full of honest feeling hammered out to captivate your soul.

*

I can sense you growing restive, impatient with my obvious maneuverings,
        so while you read this poem
I'm trying to read you—spectral partner on which everything depends—who really
  shapes
        this poem,
the way it moves and how it moves, in what directions, each line,
        each stanza
offered up for your approval like some ghostly manager obsessed with quality control,
        some god
to whom the smoke of many failures, many disappointments, straggles up to foul your
  nose.

*

And yet that first, frail poem—its pure ambition to enfold some truth, a penetrating
    glimpse
        at something
universal and profound—such lyric beauty conjured up to stir the fountains of affection
        in your heart,
the way that poem is buried in the lines of this one, as if these lines were really strokes
    of ink
        scratching out
the pristine words with which I once began, this fiftieth attempt at second-guessing
        what I thought I meant
in order to enlist your praise, leaving me to wonder what I'm doing, and where it will all
    end.

Kurt Brown (1944-2013) was founding director of the Aspen Writers' Conference, now in its 37th year, founding director of Writers' Conferences & Centers (a national association of directors) now in its 23rd year, past editor of *Aspen Anthology* and past President of the Aspen Writers' Foundation. He served on the board of Sarabande Books for many years, and on the board of Poets House in New York for six years.

His poems have appeared in many literary periodicals, including *The Ontario Review, The Berkeley Poetry Review, The Southern Poetry Review, The Massachusetts Review, The Indiana Review, The Harvard Review, Ploughshares, Kansas Quarterly, Crazyhorse*, and *Rattapallax*.

He was the editor of three annuals: *The True Subject*, Graywolf Press (1994), *Writing it Down for James*, Beacon Press (1995), and *Facing the Lion*, Beacon Press (1996) which gather outstanding lectures from writers' conferences and festivals as part of the Writers on Life & Craft Series. He was also the editor of *Drive, They Said: Poems about Americans and Their Cars* (1994), *Verse & Universe: Poems about Science and Mathematics* (1998), and co-editor with his wife, poet Laure-Anne Bosselaar, of *Night Out: Poems about Hotels, Motels, Restaurants & Bars* (1997), all from Milkweed Editions. In addition, he was the editor of *The Measured Word: On Poetry & Science*, from the University of Georgia Press in 2001, and a co-editor of the tribute anthology for the late William Matthews, *Blues for Bill*, published by University of Akron Press in 2005. He was also co-editor of *Conversation Pieces: Poems that Talk to Other Poems*, from Alfred A. Knopf (Everyman's Library Pocket Series, 2007). A new anthology, co-edited with Harold Schechter, entitled *Killer Verse: Poems about Murder & Mayhem*, was published in the Everyman's Library series in 2011.

He was the author of six chapbooks: *The Lance & Rita Poems*, which won the Sound Post Press competition in Columbia, Missouri (1994); *Recension of the Biblical Watchdog*, which won the Anamnesis Poetry Chapbook Competition (1997); *A Voice in the Garden: Poems of Sandor Tádjèck* published by Beyond Baroque Literary / Arts Center (1998); *Mammal News*, Pudding House Press (2000); *Fables from the Ark*, which won the Woodland Press

Poetry Chapbook Competition (2002), and *Sincerest Flatteries: A Little Book of Imitations*, published by Tupelo Press in the Masters' Series (2007).

His first full-length collection of poems, *Return of the Prodigals*, was published by Four Way Books in 1999. A second collection, *More Things in Heaven and Earth*, was published by Four Way Books in 2002. A third collection, *Fables from the Ark*, which won the 2003 Custom Words Prize, was published by WordTech, and a fourth, *Future Ship*, was published by Red Hen Press in 2007, followed by a fifth volume, *No Other Paradise*, in 2010. His newest collection, *Time Bound*, is out from Tiger Bark Press.

Lost Sheep: A Portrait of Aspen in the '70s, a memoir describing the town during a crucial period in its history, was published by Conundrum Press in 2012; and *Eating Our Words: Poets Share Their Favorite Recipes* is due out from Tupelo Press in 2013.

A book of translations, with his wife Laure-Anne Bosselaar, entitled *The Plural of Happiness: Selected Poems of Herman de Coninck*, was published in the Field Translation Series in 2006.

He taught poetry workshops and craft classes at Sarah Lawrence College in Bronxville, New York and served as the McEver Visiting Chair in Writing at Georgia Tech in Atlanta, Georgia and was a visiting writer at Westminster College in Salt Lake City, Utah. He taught at UCSB in Santa Barbara.

Kurt was an editor for the online journal, *MEAD: The Magazine of Literature and Libations*.

David Kirby

John the Conqueror

In the kitchen, the women are saying things I don't
        understand: *he was as mad as a mule chewing bumblebees,*
    she's as happy as a dead pig in the sunshine, you're so
stuck up you'd drown in a rainstorm. And they'd talk
        about other women, like my mother's Aunt Julia,
    who wasn't her real aunt but who worked in my grandfather's

house for years, ministering to the farm animals
        and the humans, too, when they had a touch
    of the dropsy or just weren't feeling well. And once
the women were talking about another woman, one
        they knew, or it might have been a woman in a song,
    and she was a big woman, and she'd done something

only big women do or maybe something that all women
        do, though she'd done it in such a big way that she'd
    been arrested, but when her case came up, she *shook it*
so fine for the judge that he let her go and sent the cops
        to jail, and while I didn't know what *shook it* meant
    or even what *it* was, I knew the women in the kitchen

were talking about something more powerful
        than anything I'd come across yet in my short life,
    something I'd find out about later, when I was a man,
if then. Aunt Julia wore two corsets, the one to do
        what any corset does and the other to hold all the plants
    and shoots in her backwoods pharmacy, from the alfalfa

leaf that prevents poverty to the tonka beans that stop
        your enemy's heart and the white sage that keeps your
enemy from stopping yours, and of these, there was none
more powerful than the herb the women called John
        the Conqueror that would make the one you love
love you and that took its name from an African prince

who was sold as a slave, though his spirit was never
        broken, and who survives in folklore as a trickster
of the type who appears in the works of the Zora Neale
Hurston who said he is like King Arthur of England,
        that is, not dead at all but waiting to return when
his people call him. Late in life, the Freud who called himself

a godless Jew embraced monotheism because belief
        in many gods meant you had to invoke a hundred of them
every day to banish spells, open locked boxes, get a man's
attention, win at cards. No, no, better to believe in a single
        deity, as the Jews do; this allowed them to see
the Big Picture, Freud said, and make advances in difficult fields

like law and medicine. John the Conqueror, if I had to pick
        one god, it'd be you. Not only would you lead me to love
but you'd also help me avoid the bad love that can look
like good love until it's too late. And you'd help me love
        myself as much as did the mother of, yes, the Sigmund
Freud who said there was no advantage in life greater

than being the first-born male child of a Jewish mother, who,
        in his case, dandled him on her knee and called him *mein*
goldener Sigi. My golden Siggy: what words could be
sweeter on a child's ear? In the kitchen, the women laugh
        about their own mothers and how old-fashioned
they were and how they'd complain about the women's friends,

whom they considered "fast," and say things like *look at her,*
      she's putting on that beauty makeup and *she's just*
wearing that brassiere so her bosoms will stick out
and men will look at her and *you can bait a trap*
      with meat, honey, yet you ain't gonna catch
nothing but a dog. John the Conqueror, you're my Jewish mother.

You're my Aunt Julia. You're my big woman,
      even though you're a man. Your Latin binomial
is Ipomoea purga, for you work as a strong laxative
if taken internally, and you are not to be confused with
      either Low John or Trillium grandiflorum,
      which provides assistance with family matters, or Chewing John,

that is, Alpinia galanga, of which it is said that
      if you spit its juice on the floor of a courtroom before
the judge enters, you'll win your case, which makes me
think that the big woman who *shook it* for the judge did
      something more than *shake it.* In the kitchen, the women
say *you can put a cat in an oven, but it won't lay biscuits.*

They say *why are you smiling like a goat in a briarpatch,*
      he's as useful as a screen door on a submarine,
her pants were so tight I could see her religion.
John, there have been times in my life when I might have
      called you out of the swamp, watched you step
past the sleeping birds until you reached me and took my hand.

Where are we going? You don't even know what I want.
      Out on the lake, we hear the loon's cry, long
and mournful; it says, *I'm here—where are you?* You start
to speak, and I don't know what you're saying, but I think
      you mean *wait, wait, listen,* and then,
sure enough, from the other shore, there's an answer.

Gnürszk

When people ask you where you were and you say,"Poland!"
they always say, "Did you go to Gnürszk?" and you say,
　　　"Actually, I went everywhere but Gnürszk," and they say,
"Oh, you should have gone to Gnürszk—the food there
　　　is terrific, and it's free, and it's served by beautiful naked
people, and they give you money when you leave,"
　　　and you think, Why didn't we go to Gnürszk?

No, we just went to Malbork where we saw the Castle
of the Teutonic Order, the largest castle in the world
　　　as well as the largest brick building in Europe. And then we
strolled through Warsaw's Old Town with its alleys, squares,
　　　and cosy cafés. We admired the wealth of artwork,
sculptures and silverware in Krakow's Czartorysky Museum,
　　　and in the countryside, we were grateful for the pleasant

landscapes, plentiful wildlife, and unique bird watching
opportunities. But we never made it to Gnürszk, where candy
　　　canes grow on trees and the canals are filled
with lemonade, where roasted pigs wander about with knives
　　　in their backs to make carving easy, cooked fish fall
from the sky, grilled ducklings fly directly into your mouth,
　　　the temperature is always 78 degrees, the streets are paved

with pastry, there are no clocks. If you say you went
to Germany or Italy or France, people always want to know
　　　if you went to Schnitzelkeit or Benzolio or Oisou-sur-Mer,
and you say no, no, you never made it to those places, either.
　　　But I was with the one person I wanted to be with most,
someone who loves movies and parties and books
　　　as much as I do, and even though it was a short trip,

we made love three times. Or was it four? Maybe it wasn't
any at all. Maybe if we'd gone to Gnürszk, we'd have had
        wall-socket sex, the kind that shatters the bed, blows out
the windows, breaks the pipes in the bathroom
        and floods the room below. Still, we had a good time.
Or did we? What is love, anyway? In 1982, a dentist named
        Barney Clark became the first human recipient of an artificial

        heart. The night before the operation, the doctors asked his wife
if she had any questions, and she said, yes—when you replace
        his heart, will he still love me, and the doctors said yes,
of course he will, of course, of course. Maybe we'll go
        to Gnürszk next year or the year after that. Maybe,
as the afternoon softens and turns to evening, the people
        of Gnürszk will look out their windows and wish they were us.

David Kirby's books include The House on Boulevard St.: New and Selected Poems, *a finalist for the 2007 National Book Award. His biography* Little Richard: The Birth of Rock 'n' Roll, *was hailed by* The Times Literary Supplement of London *as a "hymn of praise to the emancipatory power of nonsense." His latest book of poetry is* The Biscuit Joint. *He is the Robert O. Lawton Distinguished Professor of English at Florida State University.*

Chris Tarry

Paint Your Children Red

Last night, my oldest drove a stolen car though a plate-glass window down at the Hardee's on Main Street. I should have let him sit in jail for a week. But I didn't. I bailed him out. Walked in, laid down twenty grand, because that's what you do. Parenting 101.

And while I was driving him home, his body all slouched over in the passenger seat and staring out the window in that smartass fucking way that he does, he asked me to pull over. Said he still had drugs in his system and needed to throw up. So I eased the car over to the side of the highway and helped him down into the ditch beside the road. I held the hair on the back of his head while he puked into the long grass. Then he looked up at me, drugged out, puke all over his face, and laughed. He made the shape of a gun with his hand and pointed it toward me. *You little fucker*, I thought, *what did I do to deserve this?* He pulled an imaginary trigger with a flick of his finger, and instantly, I was back there. Ten years ago, in the garage wrestling the kids' car seats out of the back of the mini van when my wife tells me that my mother's on the phone. "She wants to ask you about your dad's sixtieth," my wife said.

"And?" I said.

"And how do I know," she said. "I'm scraping Play-Doh off the fucking walls. Ask her yourself."

When I got to the phone Mom told me my brother was planning a party for Dad.

"Dad hates birthdays," I said.

"Your brother thinks it's a good idea," said Mom.

"Since when do you listen to him?" I asked.

"Well *I'm* not planning it," she said. "How do I know what *The Boys* like?"

The Boys she called us—me, my brother, my dad—the club she could never join. When my mother would ask my brother and me to put down the toilet seat, we ignored her. When she asked my father if he could clear a little space for her craft table in the guest room, the three of us would stack more shit in there without even thinking about it. We didn't do it intentionally; at least I don't think so. But it was a team mentality, and the weight of us, *The Boys* united, made sure our team always won.

My brother and I played football with the fine china. Rode our border collie around the house like a horse until he collapsed and was never the same. When it came to helping out, we were invisible. We didn't once help with the dishes. "You two have shit for brains," Dad would tell us, then be outside an hour later, shooting hoops with us in the driveway as Mom watched from the window with a book in her lap. I didn't know how to fold a pair of pants until I was twenty-one, even today I still do it wrong. When my wife asks me to "Just pick up your goddamned towel," I say, "What towel?" because I honestly don't remember, and she's already picked it up.

There were the Penny Wars. My brother and I and a jar of loose change that lived beside the phone. I ran around the house while he tried to peg me from a distance. It took ten minutes to render the drywall in the living room ruined, my mother's vintage stemware destroyed. Dad grounded us for a month for that one but snuck us out on weekends while Mom got her hair done. We were the go-to forwards on our little-league soccer team and he hated to lose.

Then there was the time my father forgot to shut down the water to the house before our annual winter vacation. The pipes froze. My mother's homemade quilts were floating in the basement like lily pads when we got home. Dad told us he'd been grounded in ways we were too young to understand. "Stay out of your mother's way for awhile," he said.

My brother was hell on wheels and there wasn't anything he wouldn't do. And when he did whatever crazy-ass stupid thing he was thinking, he usually included me in the festivities.

"We're having a party, Fucknuts," he said to me one day. We were both in high school and Mom and Dad were on a business trip. That party ended with Danny Trentmyer's head through the living room wall after he tried to kiss Susan Smith, my brother's girlfriend at the time. I slept with Camile Henderson in my parents' bed that night; my brother gave me the condom. She was my first. To this day I can still see her gripping the top of my parents' headboard. We would have gotten away with the whole thing too, the entire party, if my brother hadn't decided to pull Mom's car from the garage and slam it into a tree in front of Susan Smith's house three blocks away.

"Talk to them, Jerry," my mother told Dad when they returned home. She was crying into her hands and sitting on the living room couch, the same couch my brother had just paid two hundred dollars to have steam cleaned.

"We can't leave you two alone for five fucking minutes," my father said, and then asked my brother what went wrong with Susan Smith.

"It's over,"my brother said. "That's too bad," said Dad, and he put his hand on my brother's shoulder. "I really liked her."

Mom looked at the three of us, shook her head, and walked out of the room.

"What the fuck is he thinking?" my wife asked when we got word that my brother picked paintball for Dad's party.

"Fun for *The Boys*," I said.

"*The Boys*. I'm so sick of the fucking boys. You'd follow that moron brother of yours to the end of the Earth," she said, and she was probably right.

My brother had joined the army at twenty-one and all it did was take his intensity and wrap it in a crew cut and a uniform Dad liked to call "mature-looking."

"That mother of yours deserves a fucking medal," my wife said. I was in the living room watching TV with a beer in my hand, feet up on the coffee table. Toys were all over the floor. "The three of you must have been a real goddamned picnic," she said.

"I wasn't so bad," I told her. "I was the good one."

She walked around the room picking up whatever I'd managed to drop on the floor. "You done with your beer Mr. Goodone? Can I get you anything else?"

I looked up at my wife. She had a toy truck in one hand and the socks I'd been wearing in the other. "I was playing with the kids," I said.

"Yeah? Well look at you," she said. "Father of the year."

The whole party thing kind of snuck up on us. Like everyone wanted to suggest a different birthday plan but forgot. Before I knew it I was driving my minivan to a place called Paintball Arena. As usual, my wife stayed home with the kids. She said that every time she saw my parents she felt a little more sorry for my mother and even more sorry for herself.

"What do you mean by that?" I said.

"Just go to your paintball game," she said.

I fell asleep in my clothes and my brother woke up in the bathtub the next morning. I still don't know what my parents worked out that night. I do know that my father wasn't one for apologizing.

The opportunities to separate *The Boys* were rare, and whenever my mother could get me alone, she did, mostly because I was the only one that ever listened to her. "Don't ever get married," she told me one day while we sat alone in the kitchen eating a bucket of ice cream. "Your dreams become a distant memory." It didn't occur to me she meant her dreams. Sometimes my mother would look at me when *The Boys* were together, single me out and just watch. Like she wanted to scoop me up and make a break for the train station.

There was this time she woke us in the middle of the night, her coat on, our tennis shoes in her hand.

"Put these on," she said. I must have been all of five years old.

"Where are we going?" my brother asked.

"Just do what I say," she said. "Downstairs. Coats on. Now."

"Where's Dad?" I asked, but she didn't answer.

"Everything's going to be OK," she said. "Just hurry."

"I'm not going anywhere with you," my brother said, and ran into the hallway bathroom and locked the door.

Then my Dad came home. You could hear him stumbling around

downstairs. It was three in the morning and he was drunk.

"Stay here and get dressed," Mom said to me. "I'll be right back."

I fell asleep in my clothes and my brother woke up in the bathtub the next morning. I still don't know what my parents worked out that night. I do know that my father wasn't one for apologizing.

In high school my brother started lifting weights and selling the steroids that helped him do it. By eighteen he could bench two-eighty-five. He'd sit at the dinner table and take down all the food you could throw at him. "The human garbage can," Dad called him, and that was the truth. He was like a refrigerator with arms. I was on the track team and everyone wanted faster times. I made my brother a good $250 a week and he gave me a cut for my troubles.

So when Garth Sterling's mother called our house after she found Garth's stash, Mom's suspicions were confirmed. She answered the phone that day. I was on the couch watching TV when I heard the phone hit the floor. I guess Mrs. Sterling laid into her pretty good. When Mom confronted my brother over dinner that night he upended the kitchen table with one hand and walked out the front door. My father spent three hours in the car looking for him. I was in bed when I heard them come home. Mom was on my brother as soon as they walked in the door. Dad told her to relax, that he'd taken care of it. "Like you take care of everything else, Jerry?" she said.

"She's wiggin'," my brother said to me later. He was laughing when he said it.

"What did Dad say?" I asked.

"What he always says," he said.

"Why are you so hard on Mom?" I asked.

"Why am *I* hard on her?" my brother said, and then gave me this look like, *You're fucking kidding me, right?* "I'm gonna' bolt," he said, and put on his coat.

"Wait, where are you going?" I asked. "Can I come?"

"Whatever," he said.

The paintball place was on the outskirts of town in a row of buildings that looked like an abandoned chemical factory. It was a Wednesday night, so we were the only ones there. The guy at the front desk suggested we break up into teams. "Parents versus kids," said my brother, and he pulled me by the arm toward the equipment area. I could see the disappointment in Dad's face.

They fitted the four of us in full-body gear and helmets with dark goggles that made everyone look like they were about to ride Motocross. My mother was smiling as she pulled on the protective pants and chest armor. "I'm so happy to see your brother taking some initiative," she said to me. "What a wonderful idea for a party."

We walked though this giant garage door into a black room with twenty-foot ceilings. Plywood mazes surrounded the perimeter. They'd given us a map of the place beforehand. "We'll give you a one minute head start," my brother said, and my parents shuffled off into the darkness.

My brother got Army real quick. Crouched down low and pointed into his eyes with both fingers like on TV. Then he motioned for me to follow, so I did.

We were walking around this maze, the room all black and streaked with dried paint. Every five minutes dry ice was released into the space and it made the air heavy with wet smoke. The music was unbelievably loud. AC/DC "Thunderstruck," I think. My brother and I were crouched behind a rectangular Styrofoam block the size of a small car when we saw my father stand up and pull off his helmet. "I've had enough of this music!" he yelled, and then abandoned my mother for the concession stand. We couldn't have been in there more than ten minutes.

The room went silent except for the sound of my mother crying. I stood to try and see where it was coming from. "Mom?" I whispered into the room. And then the music started back up again. So loud that I didn't hear the shot.

"This is gonna' be too easy," my brother said, and then rolled head over heels into the middle of the room like he was in Vietnam or some shit. Mom took him out first. Quick and efficient, like she'd been thinking about it since the day he was born. Like she knew every thought inside his ridiculous head.

"Fuck," my brother said. "Motherfucker, she got me." And then he handed me the map and left to join Dad. You could see the concession stand through a pane of glass on the far end of the room. I saw Dad give my brother a hug when he walked in.

I found a corner, sat down, pulled out the map. My brother had written *Flanking Maneuvers* in the margin and then drawn arrows between various points in the room. He'd sketched two stick figures on the page with the word *Victory!* scribbled over top.

I held my paintball gun close. The music stopped for a few seconds, the time it took for a CD to jump to the next track. The room went silent except for the sound of my mother crying. I stood to try and see where it was coming from. "Mom?" I whispered into the room. And then the music started back up again. So loud that I didn't hear the shot. It caught me hard in the left shoulder. I tripped over my feet and fell backwards. And then in an instant she was standing over me, all helmet and dark goggles so I couldn't see her face. She stepped on my chest with one foot. Her boots were thick and heavy. Paint was all over the floor.

She shot me six times, the first in my leg, maybe for the pain of childbirth and everything that would come next. Then three in my chest, probably for the sadness of seeing me turn out like my father. One in my hand, covering it in red paint. I remember looking at it and thinking, *I can barely see my wedding ring.* And then she pulled the gun up so close I could hear the barrel come to rest on my helmet. She waited. Long enough to let me know that I deserved what I got, and that no one ever gets what they think they got coming to them.

And as my kid puked beside that highway, tears streaming down our faces, I thought about that. About *my* choices. My life. And how I could hear my mother laughing as she pulled the trigger. A quick ruthless shot to the head for the pain of loving me so much.

Chris Tarry is a Canadian writer and musician living in Brooklyn. His fiction has appeared in The Literary Review, On Spec, The G.W. Review, PANK, Bull Men's Fiction, Monkeybicycle, *and elsewhere. His nonficiton has appeared in the anthology* How To Expect What You're Not Expecting; Outside In Literary & Travel Magazine; *and other cool places. In 2012, his story* "Here Be Dragons," *was nominated for a Pushcart Prize. Chris holds an MFA in creative writing from the University of British Columbia, and is a four-time Juno Award winner (the Canadian Grammy). He is also considered one of New York's most sought-after bass players. His debut story collection* How To Carry Bigfoot Home *is forthcoming from Red Hen Press in Spring 2015. www.christarrywriting.com*

Adam Vines

The Hipster Pragmatist and the Emo Poet Blunt Their Teeth after Three Bottles of Mad Dog 20/20 and Adequate Sex

Leaves are more than just leaves—
arbitrary as the arbitrary
letters that invoke them, the letters
suspended, arranged; and, again, suspended
like quivering arrows until bent for meaning like
infinite sets collecting and scattering the infinite.

Leaves are just that: leaves—
matted in a gutter, not matted
by the gutter and christened conceptual found-art, a good-bye
some lame artist names "The Parts of its Sum,"
not an island colonially clear-cut, not
a snake eating its tail, not one anchored "A"
damming the watershed of animus, not some eternal damning.

Crosses are just that: crosses—
electric chairs painted white; electric
white like Good Friday is only white
while the walls of the church, the white wile
congregating in pews loses interest in the sermon. Congregating
crows beyond the crazed glass catch their eyes. "Eat a murder of crows,"
they think, then ask, "who are these "brothers and sisters" of mine, I, we,
    they?"
We are more than just that: we—
two quarks, dualities of light, we, one, two,
blue haze before we burn blue.

No Wake Zone

Another fish camp has been razed, bait store,
crab shack. The pilings from their old piers
flaunt oyster-swollen knees at low tide.
Three stories have built up next to the landing
where I once launched my boat,
a sprawl of condos on the other side.
But for now in the no wake zone
before the mouth of the channel,
an old salt cast-nets a few mullet for the smoker.
A man sculls a girl wearing her snorkel
through the deep swells from yachts
and out to the grass flats for scallops,
and perched on a cypress knee, Old Smokey—
a heron with one eye—recognizes my misfiring Merc
in a channel of smooth four-strokes and inboards
and flies to the old buoy where I pitch my leftover bait.

Adam Vines is an assistant professor of English at the University of Alabama at Birmingham, where he is editor of Birmingham Poetry Review. *He has published recent poems in* Poetry, Southwest Review, 32 Poems, Gulf Coast, redivider, The Literary Review, *among others. His collection of poetry is* The Coal Life *(University of Arkansas Press). The Alabama State Council on the Arts awarded him a 2013 Individual Artist Fellowship. He has received awards for his teaching from the University of Florida and the University of Alabama at Birmingham.*

David Blair

Lucy Days

I am sorry
for feigning
personhood
so many times
before I was one.
The sun falls
on the grass
poking snow,
kind of irritating,
the directions
also absurd,
high-pleated
archaic fat man pants,
to make us walk
like Fred Mertz
until it hurts.

The Week of Bombs

I tell my friend anything on Beacon.

That I found 1983 beach novels so sexy
with embossed letters and vertical cracks,
the alphabet of love, for horn dog kids.

That I freak out all night about different things
and feel glad that the birds make a racket.

Days after the bombs, we drive around town
and are still hopeless sad jokers,
still starting a strange momentum.

W.C. Fields is still funny. Og Oggilby is.
The whole look of cowboy boots
and sundresses seems good for the human spirit.

I remember a lady who put one boot on a trunk
and pulled her dress over head
with practically no hands.
Her boots were blue
and her hair was brown.

I would rather lose one arm
than a leg, but would take two
arms over two legs. Who gets to choose?
The talk, the actions, the deeds, the desires
are all that remain, the important stuff.
The glove compartment is a good idea.

To say otherwise is a demonstration.

End to End New Jersey

Up north, the dead are buried nose to nose
the way cars are parked in the Oranges,
and the downspouts and metal awnings
are edge to edge, Godfather-looking style
in the parking of the dead. Down the other tip,
the motels are the same way,
with the swimming pools lifted up
over more parking, welcoming French Canadians
to the warm waters, the humid fisheries,
artificial palms.

Everybody says the sanderlings
run, true, but closer: they are splayed triangles.
You would stay longer with the two kinds of egrets,
if the bugs would stop biting, and the Great Blue Heron
stood out in the middle of the pool like a solitary Yao Ming
in an airport. Of course, with all of this marsh grass
filling the channel in, that is exactly what this is for birds.

Meanwhile, the preacher in the freaky boardwalk chapel
at the electric piano amid the empty folding chairs,
he is probably thinking with quaint categories
or cotton candy, maybe slices of pizza, too.
I would go odd or even myself at the carny.

In the water, people think about the fishes.
Empty pools most of the day. You're too early
and too late. Absent presences, birders know
the pressure of continuous music.

Where does the lumber come from?
It comes from somewhere, the wood
they make outdoor showers out of,
and the wood that holds the screens together
and the planks of the porches, too. Ask ospreys.

I practically walked across the channel to Wildwood,
was out as far as the humped toll booth
on the two lane bridge,
under the restoration of the clouds
thanks to regenerative principles
and that you always pay as we go.

David Blair's first book Ascension Days *was chosen by Thomas Lux for the Del Sol Poetry Prize in 2007. His poems have recently appeared in* Agni, InDigest, Ploughshares, Slate Magazine *and* Boston Review. *He teaches at the New England Institute of Art in Brookline, Massachusetts.*

Daniel Nathan Terry

Elegy for a Marriage

I

Each morning the hen crows like a rooster, plays the role
of harbinger and husband, filling in the gaps with a primal cry,
half-warning, half-lamentation. She cocks her yellow eye

to heaven. Her look interrogates the clouds, forces the revelation
of a broad-winged hawk. It circles twice, rides the updrafts
into some other's last morning.

II

Your wife cannot walk on her own
now. Lies there day after day.

Her eyes still accuse you for being
the man you are, they still shout

but when she tries to speak,
she mews like a brambled wren.

The arms that gathered eggs,
that held you, sometimes, at bay

are X'd on her chest. So
the couch seems already

her coffin, or it would
if her fingers

weren't in constant motion.
Though empty, they worry

each other as if something
is between them.

III

The rainbowed bantam, jungle-sleek,
with the checkered nape of a Dominique,
secrets her infertile eggs in the weedy thicket

far from the rotting coop that's become
a skull—black socket-windows
and an open maw.

IV

The deep woods you loved
have been sold, logged, stripped,

the forest floor ravaged
to pay doctors who can do nothing

but prolong pain.
Even the century oaks

just past the gate—where she sat
those after the fight afternoons,

naming the birds in whispers—
are gone, proving that despite your memory,

they were never yours.
Eventually everything is lost,

winnowed away,
stolen in one stroke, unless wisely

surrendered.

V

Spring storm and the roar of the creek. In darkness
a lady's slipper dislodges from the bank and is swept
into the knotted roots of a river oak, miles away.

Furrows flood. A vole quits his muddy burrow,
scrambles into the tangled shelter of last year's
squash and cucumber vines. He nestles down

in blackness, inhales the first green threads
of life just breaking ground. Your neglect,
to him, more useful than your best effort.

VI

Today she drums her breast like a warrior,
settles back upon her nest among the weeds that surrender
the laboring breath of Confederate Violets,

as she futilely anticipates tiny earthquakes, fractures
in the alabaster shells—life beaking its way back to the farm.
She watches you standing at the edge of the field,

the tin bucket of dinner scraps growing heavy in your hand.

VII

Beneath the oak's ghost—
a sapling maple.

Even as sixty-eight years of marriage
in the hollows in the Appalachians decay,
as she lies wordless, dying, ferns
uncurl from the rotting logs.

A rooster from an adjacent farm
finds his way into the valley
and crows from the returning ironwoods.
The hen turns her eggs.

Sweetbriar stretches from the shadows
and hooks onto the wounds of light
the felled trees have opened in the canopy. Blood
trilliums beat again in the undergrowth.

Against your will,
life comes down the hill,
through the shattered forest—
scattering beauty.

Relentless.

Unforgiving.

City of Crows

Too cold for camellias. White flowers burn to parchment
beneath the pines, beneath the retreating hounds

of the night, the remains of the moon still hanging
in the warm illusion of the brightening sky. I don't want

to remain in my dead garden, don't want to
walk upon the frozen ground, even in my shoes.

My coat is too thin, but I don't want walls around me.
The crows of dawn agree, are adamant; they urge

me over the fields beyond the sadness of this neighborhood.
Even the houses of the poor, they insist, are beautiful

from the winter sky. But what kind of man follows
the advice of crows? They say the earth is not eternal,

that work is useless, that this day is already someone's last.
Wander, wander, they insist. Someone has lost something needed.

Someone else has thrown away love. From the top of the city,
we will come upon these both, and these are all we require.

Daniel Nathan Terry, a former landscaper and horticulturist, is the author of four books of poetry: City of Starlings *(forthcoming from Sibling Rivalry Press, 2015);* Waxwings *(2012);* Capturing the Dead, *which won The 2007 Stevens Prize; and a chapbook,* Days of Dark Miracles *(2011). His poems and short stories have appeared, or are forthcoming, in numerous publications, including* Cimarron Review, The Greensboro Review, New South, Poet Lore, *and* Southeast Review. *He serves on the advisory board of One Pause Poetry and teaches English at the University of North Carolina in Wilmington, where he lives with his husband, painter and printmaker, Benjamin Billingsley.* http:// danielnathanterry.com/

Terrance Hayes

Palmetto State

South Carolina? It reminds of that *that*
That kinetic brats cry in the Lexington flea market
Saturday free-for-alls, a greed that strays

Between the flawed merchandise merchants hawk
And famers' ruffage and ham hocks—the boiled
Peanuts, my lord, meat is tender in a shell!

Terrance Hayes was a cap gun with no caps.
He was an uncaught catchphrase awaiting a net.
He flopped like a catfish in his father's clutch.

And I sigh, what's the use: too soon the Saluda River
Will be mist. South Carolina, you are in love with Bluff
Estates, Negros, captains and catastrophes.

I will visit you when snow falls on the north and leave
My children mouthing the church hymns I failed
To teach them. They will be bark-toned and tone

Death, and know less than I know of 1865,
Main Street, Columbia, mourning after the burning.
Legislatures of a magnificent malfunctioning

Manufacturing history. The self can't work
On the self alone: distant roads are needed.
I am homesick for the motels of Caesar's Head.

I want to find someone who has never owned
Nor consumed anything American: a Catawba Indian,
A Goose Creek gypsy. In the flea market

Terrance failed to flee poverty and was hooked by the arms
Of a territorial Beulah, his 200 plus pound round
Grandmother in an antique blouse. If I say "I love you" more

Than "I hate you," if I say, "I love you" several times
A day it will accumulate truth, South Carolina.
Mother, nature, God, father, grade school, bully, pulpit.

Hell's misspelled angles. A place as paradoxical
As chocolate imported from the Congo: South Carolina.
A place the tongues are made of gold, rumor, crabgrass.

I have reliable information from people who are close
To other people. All my teachers are dead.
All my lovers are dead. Terrance Hayes slept in a motel

With a bullet in the gun on his pillow and is dead.
The brand new Bible he found was a black and tender
Leather, but his mother kept saying it needed to be read.

American Sonnet for Wanda C.

Who I know knows why all those lush boned worn out girls are
Whooping at where the moon should be, an eyelid clamped
On its lightness. Nobody sees her without the hoops firing in her
Ears because nobody sees. Tattooed across her chest she claims
Is BRING ME TO WHERE MY BLOOD RUNS and I want that to be
   here
Where I am her son, pent in blackness and turning the night's calm
Loose and letting the same blood fire through me. In her bomb hair:
Shells full of thunder, in her mouth the fingers of some calamity,
Somebody foolish enough to love her foolishly. Those who could hear
No music weren't listening—and when I say it, it's like claiming
She's an elegy. It rhymes, because of her, with effigy. Because of her
If there is no smoke, there is no party. I think of you, Miss Calamity,
Every Sunday. I think of you on Monday. I think of you hurling hurt
where the moon should be and stomping into our darkness calmly.

Terrance Hayes, is the author of four books of poetry; Lighthead *(2010), winner of the 2010 National Book Award in Poetry;* Wind in a Box, *winner of a Pushcart Prize;* Hip Logic, *winner of the National Poetry Series, a finalist for the Los Angeles Times Book Award, and runner-up for the James Laughlin Award from the Academy of American Poets, and* Muscular Music, *winner of both the Whiting Writers Award and the Kate Tufts Discovery Award.*

Stuart Dischell

Looking for Robert Desnos:

State of Alert: the Last Transformation of the Surrealist Poet

Walking along the rue de Bagnolet near the eastern edge of Paris, I stepped into la Fleche d'Or, a club and café established in what had been

Robert Desnos

a station of the Petit Ceinture, the old circular railway. Near the back windows, people at tables and chairs looked out over the industrial peace of overgrown tracks. A semi-circular bar closed off a serving area. The rest of the space was empty except for the black boxes of sound equipment and two low wooden stages. On the walls someone had sprayed totemic graffiti patterns similar to those in downtown clubs in New York in the early eighties. I stood at the bar and ordered a Belgian beer from the tap with an aftertaste initially reminiscent of varnish.

The open-faced young woman serving drinks and coffee wore her hair up in a net-like cap the way a Rastafarian does. She had on a long, tan skirt that concealed her legs and made her appear kind of like a mermaid in her embroidered white shirt. She used no makeup but a lot of silver rings pierced her ears and a small slender hoop went through her left nostril. Her pupils were dilated, and when she spoke I felt as if I could walk right into them. After being quiet all day it would be good to have a conversation with such a person. She was surprised that I knew a little about the old railway, the "little belt" that ran just inside what were once the city walls, which are themselves referred to as *ceintures*, "belts." Only a few vestiges remain of its twenty-nine stations—one a swank restaurant across town in La Muette.

Over the years, people have snuck onto the tracks. Ultimately, the tracks of the Petit Ceinture will be a green walk similar to the Parc Plantee or the High Line in Manhattan.

La Fleche d'Or, named after a fancy nineteenth-century train, opened in 1995 in the former Gare de Charonne. This station, closed in 1933, nearly sixty years after its construction, provides an excellent if idiosyncratic example of how a café and club can prosper in a space unsuited to other enterprises. The open waiting room is perfect for performances, and the lower area track side used for storage, private parties, and the overflow crowd on the weekends. At two thirty in the afternoon in the middle of the week, though, only a few people sat out by the glass-enclosed area drinking coffee and reading newspapers and books and no one was at the bar but me, a situation that would change but not drastically. I ordered another beer.

I told the young woman how la Fleche d'Or reminded me of clubs in New York. This made her smile. She smiled a lot and spoke English well and with ease. When I had said New York, she got dreamy and I wondered if it were her desire for a different city or sorrow at the recent events of terror whose ripples could be seen in the current vigilance in Paris. Or maybe that's just how she looked. Her pupils enlarged as she spoke, and on the way in I swear I could smell pachouli.

The rue de Bagnolet had for centuries been the main drag of the ancient hilly village of Charonne. Jean-Jacques Rousseau, the original walker in the city, after taking his dinner on October 24, 1776 had "followed the boulevards up to the rue de Chemin-Vert then gained the heights of Menilmontant; and from there, taking the paths across the vineyards and meadows, followed as far as Charonne the smiling landscape which unites the two villages." On another occasion he was attacked by a huge farm dog.

I had come to see the street I had read about in the Robert Desnos poem "Lines of the rue de Bagnolet" from *State of Alert*, the last book published during his lifetime. I wanted to see where the sun wore a bucket for a hat,

I wanted to see where the sun wore a bucket for a hat, where the sun was like no other. It had been raining a lot and I would have been glad to see the sun at all.

where the sun was like no other. It had been raining a lot and I would have been glad to see the sun at all.

LINES OF THE RUE DE BAGNOLET

The sun of the rue de Bagnolet
Is a sun unlike the others
It bathes itself in the gutter,
It wears a bucket for a hat,
Like all the others,
But, when it rubs my shoulders,
It is itself and not another,
The sun of the rue de Bagnolet
Drives a cabriolet
Somewhere not the palace gates
Sun, sun not pretty or homely,
Sun all funny and all happy,
Sun of the rue de Bagnolet,
Sun of winter and spring,
Sun of the rue de Bagnolet,
Unlike the others.

The previous afternoon, on the other side of the river, I walked from our rental apartment near the Observatory down the rue Campagne Premiere, across boulevard Raspail, and to the entrance of the Montparnasse Cemetery on the boulevard Edgar Quinet. These cemetery walls once stood just outside the Toll Wall of 1785, a sensible practice, dating back to Roman times, of relegating corpses to the outskirts of the city. My three-year-old son was with me. The drizzle did not stop him from running up and down the alleys of graves. The sign inside the gates of the cemetery showed the Desnos tomb located in the 15th section, but it took several passes to find it positioned in the fifth row not far from section 8—good seating for a café in winter but less fortunate for eternity.

My son complained because he could not find our names on any of the tombs. He ran around but not on top of them, a bargain he made with me that involved a soft drink later. Earlier he had been out of sorts because of the rain. All the while he quarreled with his sister, I had been trying to translate "the sun unlike the others" on the rue de Bagnolet.

The *Desnos* family grave is a plain black rectangle simply marked Desnos without specific reference by first name to Robert or any of his relations. Cemetery space in Paris was always precious and I wondered about the manner in which their remains were arranged in there. Desnos had been an original Surrealist, a friend of Andre Breton, Paul Eluard, and Louis Aragon, and, like his fellows, an anti-fascist. Having been born in that remarkable generation of 1900, his great poetic periods were in the twenties and forties, the years of his own twenties and forties. He was a member of the Resistance, who may have smuggled news information out of the offices of the newspaper where he worked, and a trenchant critic of right-wing authors. He was arrested on February 22, 1944 at his home at 19 rue de Mazarine in St-Germain des Pres, delivered to the dread internment facility at rue de Saussaies where many Resistance fighters were tortured, driven to Fresnes outside of Paris, and then transported to the Camp de Royallieu a Compiegne. Two months after his arrest the authorities sent him by boxcar to Auschwitz, Buchenwald, several prison factories, then marched him across the mountains into Czecho-slovakia where he died of typhus at the Terezin concentration camp on June 8, 1944, a few weeks after the camps were liberated by the Red Army. Not a Jew but, as Celine described him, a "jew-lover," he rests among the graves of Jews and Christians in the egalitarian Montparnasse Cemetery where people of all and no faiths are still being buried. In an earlier poem in *State of Alert* he writes:

EARTH

Day after day,
Plot after plot

Where do you go? Where are you going?
The earth is bruised by so many errant men!
The earth is enriched by the corpses of so many men.
But the earth is us,
We are not on top of her
But in her since forever.

Andre Breton purged Desnos from the Surrealist movement, supposedly for writing too well, but nonetheless believed he came closest to the surrealist ideal both in his work and spirit. From the start Desnos was the most idiosyncratic, Houdini-like figure, the oracle of their gatherings. He survived manifestos, automatic writing, opium, suicide parties, his first conscription—but not the Nazis.

Not far from the Canal St-Martin in the tenth arrondissement near Mountfacon where the *gibet*, the medieval gallows, stood, Paris has named a public square for him. Still a high spot but sort of a circular courtyard among characterless modern apartments, Place Robert Desnos is the meeting point now of streets named for Handel, Camus, Francis Jammes, and the Polish poet Boy Zelenski. It is a place devoid of resonance, yet the product of the French penchant for honoring its intellectuals, somewhat fitting for the author of a book entitled, *Domaine Public*.

Desnos had no association with the Mountfacon neighborhood, however. He took apartments on the other side of the city—his wildest years were on the rue Blomet in the fifteenth arrondissement. Afterwards he lived with his wife Youki on the rue Mazarine where he was arrested. He grew up near the markets in St-Merri, a neighborhood later razed as an *ilot insalubre*, an unhealthy enclave of densely inbred alleys and streets. In the middle ages it had been known for the alchemists who resided there. Desnos' father worked as a wholesaler of beef, poultry, or game at nearby

Les Halles, a grill owner, a deputy mayor, or the operator of a café, in all respects a proper bourgeois.

Lucien Desnos' skill with the saw and knife may have made the poet adept at the dissociative as well as associative nature of surrealist art, the sharp mortal cuts.

LINES OF THE BUTCHER

If you want, my beauty, I will make a bed for you
In the bloody decor of my boutique.
My knives will be illusionary mirrors
Where the day clears, shines, and clouds.

I will make a warm bed, hollowedí
For you in the open guts of a heifer
And when you sleep you could be a young woman again.
I will watch over you like an executioner guards the scaffold.

"Lines of the Butcher" is the most macabre terrifyingly sexual of the "couplets." In many respects. It is, well, the most surreal of the poems of *State of Alert* and stands out as a vestige rather than an example of the book.

This poem along with the others published in 1943 is devastatingly simple. In the prose afterword to the collection, Desnos suggested that the poems began as automatic writing exercises composed in the thirties, which he revised in the early forties as he was writing new poems that reflected his desire to use the rhymes of Spanish couplets, Cuban rhythms that had first enticed him on a visit to Miguel Asturias in Havana for *la Prensa Latina* conference in 1928, and American blues. I believe he was also aware of the ways that Federico García Lorca, the first martyred artist of the War, had used these kinds of formal techniques to create a poetry that was both rhythmic and surreal. Desnos' work of this period had come after years of writing love poems, fables, verses for children, and more recently poems of resistance—as well as writing thousands of publicity slogans and advertisements for the radio.

State of Alert contains nineteen poems, the prose afterword, and ten engravings by the artist Gaston-Louis Roux. It was published on April 28, 1943 under the direction of Robert J. Godet and typeset by J. Grou-Radenez in an edition of 170 copies, twenty of which were not distributed for reasons of imperfection. Desnos received the first thirty, the illustrator the next ten, 41-50 went to a certain but unknown AM Payot, and the rest kept for distribution by the publisher. The collection was meant to be distributed among friends during the Occupation and was not sold in shops. It is an underground publication aptly dedicated "a mes amis," to my friends. My version is a photocopy of number 60. There is currently one available on the internet from a bookstore in the rue St-Honore for €3200.

The book opens with a bestiary, four fabulist poems regarding a camel, a bear, a bull, and a bee, followed by "Earth" and "Suicides," poems that concern the buried, "the hanged, the cut, and the poisoned." They are followed by "At Five AM" and "I Have Taken Myself Walking," a pair that reintroduces the urban landscape of the book that was suggested earlier and more fancifully in "History of a Bear" in which the bear enters the city to uproarious effect. But the poems in *State of Alert* that interest me most are the ones written during the Occupation of Paris. They roughly comprise the second half of the book, the group of six "couplets" that he thought of as little songs rather than couplets in the English rhyming sense and the concluding four poems he termed as classical in nature.

Although Desnos' poems had previously contained references to Paris, the poems of *State of Alert*, and the subsequent poems, such as "The Watchman of the Seine," that would be posthumously collected in his last volumes most concern the physical details of the city. During the Occupation, place names became touchstones, and he imbued the very statuary and bridges with the Surrealist's hypnotic powers of transformation and the summoning of political resistance. Having grown in the warren of the St-Merri and St-Martin neighborhoods, his "Lines on the rue Saint Martin" resonate not only because of the "disappearance" of Andre Platard, Desnos' friend and fellow Resistance figure, but also because of where the poem is set. It helps also to explain the repeated line, "I don't much like the rue Saint-Martin," a blues repetition which also sounds like something a hurt child might say.

LINES OF THE RUE ST-MARTIN

I don't much like the rue St-Martin
Since Andre Platard left it.
I don't much like the rue Saint-Martin,
I like nothing, not even wine.

I don't much like the rue St-Martin
Since Andre Platard left it.
He's my friend, he's my pal.
We shared a room and our bread.
I don't much like the rue Saint-Martin.

He's my friend, he's my pal.
He disappeared one morning,
They took him away, nothing is known.
Not to be seen again on the rue St-Martin.

No use praying to the saints,
Saints Merri, Jacques, Gervais, and Martin,
Not even Valerien hidden on the hill.
Time passes, nothing is known.
Andre Platard has left the rue St-Martin.

The neighborhood now exists in a one block fashion around the Church of St-Merri that was spared and in the narrow streets just south of the Pompidou Museum. You can get a feel for it by seeing a skillful macquette of how it looked in the Carnavalet Museum.

Desnos also writes of the nearby Porte St-Denis and its lesser-known, somewhat shorter neighboring gate, Porte St-Martin.

LINES OF THE PORTES
SAINT MARTIN AND SAINT DENIS

Porte Saint Martin, Porte Saint Denis
To see the moonlight pass through the arch

Porte Saint Martin, Porte Saint Denis
North to south stretches the road
Porte Saint Denis, Porte Saint Martin
North or south follows its path
Porte Saint Martin, Porte Saint Denis
To walk under the arch in the little morning
Porte Saint Martin, Porte Saint Denis
To drink black coffee with friends,
Porte Saint Martin, Porte Saint Denis
When the sky becomes white in the little morning
Porte Saint Denis, Porte Saint Martin
In the dawn to drown the ancient troubles,
To leave singing toward a far away place
With our pals, with our friends
Porte Saint Denis, Porte Saint Martin
In lovely sunshine, on a lovely morning.

Although still a dreamer, Desnos no longer poses as the sleepwalker of his early work. The sense of purposeful displacement evident in his best poems of the 1920s such as "I Have Dreamed of You" or "Like a Hand at the Moment of Death" has been replaced by a heightened sense of the city, the City of Paris, its monuments, districts, and inhabitants. The sense of place in the later poems is crucial. The voice in *Etat de Veille* is in both a state of waking consciousness and a state of being alert. The spare, almost childlike constructions harmonize with their subject. That eternal linguistic joker might have also thought the *etat de veille* is very much like *etat de ville*—the state of the city during The Occupation. Therefore I have opted to title the book in English, "State of Alert" rather than "State of Waking."

The terrible resonance of the "far way place" Desnos would end up with his *copains* creates a palpable tension that informs every movement of these poems. "Lines of the Glass of Wine" written in 1942 is hard not to read through the lens of his subsequent arrest and deportation.

LINES OF THE GLASS OF WINE

When the train leaves do not wave your hand,

Nor your handkerchief, nor your umbrella,
Instead fill a glass with wine
To throw toward the train whose ridelles sing.
The long flame of wine
Is like the same blood red flame of your tongue.
And parts like it
The palace and couch
Of your lips and mouth.

One is tempted to see box cars, freight cars or, even flat cars and hear the songs of the deported on their way to disappearing. But the fourth line of the poem, "Et lance vers le train dont chantent les ridelles," is untranslatable in American English because we do not have ridelles, the type of open, metal, cars the SNCF used in its system. You might imagine flat cars with railings. The ridelles are frequently covered with tarpaulins: the song is in the wind. The pictures I saw detailing several types of ridelles varied by the height of the supporting frame and the nature of the product to be enclosed: from lumber to vegetables were determining characteristics. The best pictures were those of hobbyist sites for toy trains. To complicate things further vers means "toward" or "to" or "at" as in its literal sense in the line, but vers is also verse. At serious play, the wine and the mouth are then poetry itself, the tongue touch of eros.

So when the girl at the former station of la Fleche d'Or told me she was off until it was time to set up the club for the night and gave me half a smile and one eyebrow rose and asked me if were remaining for another drink, my wedding ring nearly dissolved in alcohol. I never went to her place on rue de Pyrenees where we drank and smoked and I wished her housekeeping was better. I did not stay for a week and get a tattoo like the black rose on her hip. I did have a third Belgian beer, however, and I made a plan with myself to return some night to better check out la Fleche d'Or.

§ § § § §

Guillaume Apollinaire created the term "surrealism" for a performance piece in which all the arts collided, a heightened aesthetic condition. Apollinaire himself of various confused and known ancestry was a collision of peoples, the modern man of the new century whose future was beyond cartographic frontiers. He named himself after a water bottle. The early works of the Dadaists, those precursors of surrealism, involved all sorts of antics—art shows in which the viewers would fall into a pit inside a gallery, plays in which gas-filled balloons in the form of naked female breasts floated above the audience. In short, the origins of what the avant garde has been dishing up for nearly a hundred years. Its purpose was to shock, to amaze, to engage, to make the reader, the audience, the viewer participate in the altered act of consciousness. Later the movement under the leadership of Andre Breton drifted towards séance, psychoanalysis, and ultimately Communism as the events in the world caught up with the practitioners. The landscape of the movement was the streets of Paris.

When Paul Celan, who jumped off Pont Mirabeau and was not a surrealist, wrote, "they are digging a grave in the sky, there is room to lie down there" he was speaking literally as well as figuratively. The "medical" experiments of the Nazis went well beyond Luis Buñuel and Salvadore Dalí's famous slit eyeball scene in *Un Chien Andalou*. The mass graves of the camps, the photos of striped prisoners and stripped skeletons, the mounds of teeth, heaps of pots and pans, children's shoes, and looms of women's hair are an overstatement that the onlooker can no longer comprehend. Mike, an English businessman at the hotel bar in Krakow, told me, "I had seen it all before but this time it was in color."

But even the color of the death camps was essentially sepia, lightened by a few pale green trees.

The atrocities of World War II overshadowed those committed in all previous wars and the bourgeois culture to which French surrealism had reacted in the years after the First War was shattered forever. Totalitarianism, however, was another matter. For the Europeans after the War, their upheavals and dislocations created the less light-hearted literature of Sartre, Camus, Celan, Grass, and Levi.

In 2002, I would travel to Krakow and go to the Polish village of Oswiecim and walk through the gates of Auschwitz, the ugliest word in the German language, to see where Desnos had been early on incarcerated and where so many of the disappeared of Paris vanished and where my grandparents, had they remained in France, would have been incinerated. There are pictures from 1943 of the arrival of about 1700 Parisians who were tattooed with numbers, Desnos was given 185,443. I did not see his face among them. He might still have been wearing the cape his neighbor gave him to keep warm on his journey. I would visit the crematoria and photograph the ovens for myself. For months afterwards, I would become one of those people who wave horrible photos in your face. In the stillness of the stark camp with its filmed and staged displays, I would see how things are always less and more horrible than we imagine them. I was afraid people would openly weep here, that I might too, but the response I saw that afternoon was the stupefaction that comes with being overwhelmed.

Desnos was not cremated here nor was he machine-gunned on the train tracks of the adjacent Birkenau. Nor did he perish at Buchenwald or Flossberg although he had ample opportunity.

Desnos was not cremated here nor was he machine-gunned on the train tracks of the adjacent Birkenau. Nor did he perish at Buchenwald or Flossberg although he had ample opportunity. The guards at Floha nearly beat him to death when he came to the aid of a fellow prisoner. A friend remembered Desnos joking that he wanted to visit all of the camps. He held out until just after the liberation when the typhus at Terezin killed him. Many prisoners died in the heightened squalor and neglect of the last days of the war. The story goes that two Czech students who had come to aid the survivors found him barely alive. They had seen his name posted on a list of the internees. When they asked if he knew Robert Desnos, he told them, "I am Robert Desnos." They were fluent in French and had read his poems in school. They treated him for his illness, but it was too late. Starvation had done its job. He was cremated and his ashes transported to Paris and buried in the family tomb in Montparnasse where his mother and father had already been interred. His co-surrealist Paul Eluard has famously written that "there is another world but it is within this one." When he wrote it between the wars he obviously did not know the form that this world would take.

Throughout the Occupation, Desnos sought to remain hopeful, to remain engaged, to publish his poems and journalism under noms de plume, despite his demotion by the fascists at *Aujourd'hui* where he worked. Occasionally, he feared arrest, but for most of the Occupation he was in no real danger. Some say that his initial incarceration was the cruel joke of one Nazi officer getting back at a fellow Nazi officer who had professed high regard for Desnos' work. By this point of the Occupation many of the writers and artists had left Paris for New York like Breton, or the South of France like Picasso.

Guardedly he held out for a better future. One must always be alert for hope. "Tomorrow," one of the poems he termed "classical in appearance," appears before the afterward.

TOMORROW

When I am a hundred thousand, I will have the same
Strength to await you, o tomorrow, shadow of hope.
Even Time, an old man twisted by his pain,
May groan: "the morning is new, the evening new."

But for many months we have lived on edge,
The guardians of light and fire, we keep alert.
We speak softly and decipher as we can
The noises swiftly fading and lost like a game.

Now, from the bottom of the night we witness
The splendor of the day and all that it gives
If we do not sleep it is to await the dawn
Which will prove in the end we live in the present.

There is a close up picture of him shortly before his death at Terezin. He wears the wide vertical stripes of the prisoner. He is bent slightly forward. His sleeves appear to be rolled just below the elbows. Stubble has returned to his shaved head and there, dark growth spreads under his chin and at the edges of his jaw. His face is one of sorrow and exhaustion and sickness. I wish I could say that he still appears as if he will read his comrades' futures and tell jokes—but he looks like a man who has lost everything, whose death

can already be seen on his face. In "After Word to *Etat de Veille*," he concludes "it is not poetry that has to be free, it is the poet," a hideous truth his own life confirmed.

Of the group of well-known Surrealist poets, he was not among the most active in the Resistance but the only one deported by the Nazis and their collaborators. It was never clear what his role had been—possibly photographing news items from uncensored sources that were not printed by *Aujourd'hui* and passing them to the Resistance. By the time of his arrest in February 1944, he had been demoted at the paper and no longer was a lead reviewer. How much access he had to these articles at that point would be debatable. The other men that were arrested in this sweep were like himself, mostly professionals and intellectuals, non-Jews. Even the Nazis at Auschwitz seemed surprised by the harsh treatment of this group. A poet of Paris, his ashes were brought from Czechoslovakia to his parish church, St-Germain-des-Pres, for a ceremony. They arrived in a silver cocktail shaker.

§ § § § §

I never learned Robert Desnos' literal connection to the rue de Bagnolet. Maybe he had a friend or publisher here. His adult residences were in the fifteenth near Montparnasse and then from 1934–1944 at 19 rue Mazarine between rue St-Andre des Arts and the river. That building bears a very worn marble plaque above the entryway that confirms the address. Possibly he performed Resistance work in this working class quarter. It is clear in his poem that Desnos is punning off the name Bagnolet with the verb *baigner*, to bathe. He also alludes to the palace gates, those possibly being the gates to what was once the chateau of the powerful Dukes of Orleans, the Pavillon de Ermitage, a vestige down the street from La Fleche d'Or. I e-mailed a leading American scholar of Desnos and was relieved to learn that she did not know either, so I put it to rest.

During the war years Desnos' love for Paris grew more fierce. Not merely an urban poet, he became a true poet of the city, loving its pavement and human structures. Even more than Baudelaire, he became a poet of Paris.

In "Lines of the Sidewalk in Summer," a poem that appears just after "Lines of the rue de Bagnolet" in *State of Alert*, he again evokes the image of keeping watch or guarding. It is the flaneur at rest.

LINES OF THE SIDEWALK IN SUMMER

We should lie down on the sidewalk,
Warmed by the sun, washed by the sun,
In the good odor of dust
As the day departs,
Before the night comes on,
Before the first lamp is lit,
And keep watch in the gutter
For the reflections of clouds as they gather,
The red heat of the horizon
And the first star over the houses.

Over the years, the authorities have closed la Fleche d'Or because of problems on the premises, allegations concerning drugs and protection of immigrants and an angry confrontation with police. It has opened again then closed, then just as it was sold and about to reopen one more time a group of vandals destroyed the interior, causing the new owner to back out of the deal. It has since reestablished into a milder version of itself. Each year I check out its incarnation. I wonder what became of the girl who worked there and know in my heart I will never see her again, but the vaguest possibility of her interest in me ignited my daydreams.

Although the Petit Ceinture continued to operate until the 1930s, from the 1870s onward it became clear that the city walls would need to come down, a process started just after World War I and not completed until World War II began. This area after the last city wall was envisioned by urban planners as a green belt around Paris, and in portions it does in fact contain sports fields and athletic parks. A confusion over who had rights to the property also created a hodgepodge of industry, residential apartment blocks, gas stations, prostitutes, drug dealers, and wholesale supermarkets.

These are still the poorer streets of Paris and the most densely populated. There are no museums here or fashionable shops or distinguished lycées. Rent and food prices are, for now, lower than in other parts of town. The Porte de Bagnolet, an active if characterless intersection with its crust of modern structures, hides the rue de Bagnolet from the automobiles at the terrifying juncture of the auto routes and Peripherique. Above it all, the former village of Charonne retains its village air. Like the Butte–de–Cailles to the south, it is a high place where people are cool. And it is also a typical neighborhood. Paris is always revealing itself this way. Up here what you breathe does feel a little cleaner, the sun has just a little brighter quality, maybe a sun in fact unlike the others, reflecting in puddles and even maybe in that bucket just after rain.

Stuart Dischell is the author of Good Hope Road, *a National Poetry Series Selection, (Viking, 1993),* Evenings & Avenues *(Penguin, 1996),* Dig Safe *(Penguin, 2003), and* Backwards Days *(Penguin, 2007) and the chapbooks* Animate Earth *(Jeanne Duval Editions,1988) and* Touch Monkey *(Forklift, 2012). Dischell's poems have been published in* The Atlantic, Agni, The New Republic, Slate, Kenyon Review, *and anthologies including* Essential Poems, Hammer and Blaze, Pushcart Prize, *and* Garrison Keillor's Good Poems. *He has given readings from his work at hundreds of venues, including The Library of Congress, the Los Angeles Times Book Festival, The Chateau Marmont, the American Library of Paris, and the American University of Paris. A recipient of awards from the NEA, the North Carolina Arts Council, and the John Simon Guggenheim Foundation, he is a the Class of 1952 Distinguished Professor in the MFA Program in Creative Writing at the University of North Carolina Greensboro.*

Patricia Smith

It Creeps Back In

before i can focus, before i can remember
those calm bankrolled liturgies, i'm gulping
gin and sipping water, i've gone rigid in front
of an open refrigerator, spraying neon butter
into my mouth. i brush dead hair into the sink,
peer at bleeding gums and a hushed cell, sit
at the keyboard and sing, like i've been told
to, *anything that moves you toward the folding.*
i've been healed and hallelujahed countless
times, usually on tuesdays between 3 and 4,
usually by a white woman schooled in the coo.
And are you still sleeping all day?, why yes,
i am, because the night i've crafted is sugar
skirting the bounds of a murder. *Depression
should never be ignored,* the hers warn, so i
nurture the gulp, encourage the sly pink rituals
of my throat. finally opening my eyes, i rock
backwards, enter myself with a snaking finger.
i'm mightily amazed at the ghost of current.
strange how september says *i still need you,*
how it's learned to lie in the voice of a mother.

Inspection

On every inch of me, there are rumors of fathers, all of them stifling snarls behind the grinning death mask of the one who gave me name. Stubbled and siren, they have scrubbed me seriously clean of hair, pummeled my weight, wrenched my studied suburban breath from its moorings. Drowning out the organ, they coo and trumpet. slyly measuring the shrinking distance between me and the water.

I'll Call You, Okay?

Oh, goddamn
this all, cuticles chewed, unwashed hair, aspirin for lunch, the white
urgent drone of the news channel. (Somewhere, again, a tornado has
touched down, inhaling elms, ribbons of interstate.) The hell with this
perfumed crush beneath the world's rough clock, this damnable metronome
tick tick
and scrunched gaze where all that's visible is romance sporting
its shredded little coat, wildly stylish, but knowing no reason against rain.

Patricia Smith is the author of six acclaimed poetry volumes. Blood Dazzler, *which chronicles the devastation wreaked by Hurricane Katrina, was a finalist for the 2008 National Book Award.* Shoulda Been Jimi Savannah *(Coffee House Press, 2012), was a finalist for the William Carlos William Award from the Poetry Society of America. Smith is currently at work on the biography of Harriet Tubman; a collection of short fiction and a coffee table book combining poetry with 19th century photos of African Americans.*

Matt Hart

from Radiant Action

After the fall and after the flood, and after being
married for fourteen years, and after the dog
starting limping to tell us the new water heater
and the brake pads, the high blood pressure
pills, sweet heat of the sun, a Michigan
summer on loan from Ohio, the angels
and insects and Lew Welch poems
"I burn up the deer in my body"
I visit New York and Chicago   I go the whole distance,
and I never fight with anyone   Noise is the unfiltered sound
of the earth, all it is, and all we've done, all we've fucked up
but the engine purrs on   Green green green,
so I think of Walt Whitman   The Taliban talking
with the Afghan government   A bomb going BLAM
as a distant star collapses   Then a massive manhunt
launched by physicists   We listen to China at the United Nations
and the voices of children on an old wooden swingset,
one of them ours, and one of them a genius,
one of them a sparrow with an orange tree
reactor, "lovely fruit of light"   It's all the same voice
It's all the same urge   What was inanimate
is suddenly animate   "Won't you please,"
it screams from a sweater   With language
we attempt to make ourselves immortal
Noise is a reminder we aren't

*****

"I imagine you and the lake
taking long walks together"
Bob wrote that to me, so I'm taking it
and running with it   I don't walk much,
but I run, and the lake seems to like it
My shoes in the sand several miles
along the beach   The lake waves on,
its murmur undetected, its roar on the table
The dog still limping   She won't tell me
what's the matter, can't tell me what's wrong
Her facemask-nosecone so suddenly white, eleven
years old and the scenery gasping something amber
and flitting, a gold thing with what appears to be
hair-powdered wings   I don't know
what anything is really, but it isn't life or death,
that's sure   Third cup of something—
brownish water, greenish flavor   A broom
propped up on what looks like the distance
I ask the dog, now licking her paw, to tell me
what she knows, but she is overly pre-
occupied with sentience, not the sentence
"Ask one of the other girls," she squawks,
sounding more and more like something
that might fly at any minute, or maybe
like a chotchke on a shelf about to fall   I hate
the lame comparisons   The constant atmospheric
calls   Angels exist, but they aren't like
in the books   Their nature is Nature
They *are* Nature   Some of them are chained,
and some of them float   But all of them are
free   Me and the lake take long runs together,
and all we ever talk about is heaven

*****

Heaven is all I ever talk about, unless
I'm talking about hellaciousness, which is
all the rest of the time   What am I
talking about now   Most often these days,
just attentive to plethora—the sound
of waves produced by waves on the lake
At the moment it's calm and vivid
with fishing boats, the gulls taking dives,
the laugh track of a family playing,
not mine   Mine is in Pentwater,
the little town nearby, having lunch
while I finish my coffee, reading poems,
"The Crystal Lithium" by Schuyler
and "Love Love Love Again" by Philip
Whalen again   It all sounds so much better
than I mean it   If someone walked
around the corner, they could sneak
a small piece of my life into their pocket
and steal it—that is, if they could see me
and not be scared off by the dog, both of us
invisible in the lavender, soon to be
much brighter noon-ish-ness
Noise a kind of radiance, that's why
I'm absent, taking these notes, instead of
right now in Pentwater   Venous Hum,
the sound of the devil   It goes and goes
Agnes killed a slug by drowning it
accidentally   I'm sorry, little darling,
I told you it would happen   I told you,
but the summer's interference
wouldn't let you   Listen

*****

At the Michigan cottage, near Pentwater,
the back, west-facing wall of the room
where we stay is all glass, so this morning
as usual I'm looking at the lake,
its constancy, expanding and
contracting, expanding and con-
tracting, breathing in and out
for some eternity eternity
Today there's fog, because
it rained last night, so the lake
itself is almost white, bedsheet
of nothing   What there is is that
I hear it, a becalmed and calming resonance,
nothing sinister about it, the proscenium
of trees, the minutia of their movements,
their limbs upon limbs and their June green
leaves   "No birds sing" wrote Keats in a poem
and it's the absence of noise, which becomes
the sound of bad omen, something bewitched
and bewitching   The birds are quieter
than usual today, so I'm thinking of Keats
and listening to the white-washing sounds
of the lake   Thinking also about Nate,
who I'll see in a few weeks, and his suggestion
that we collaborate on a pair of essays
I'm writing one already, On Noise, and he would
write one called & Exhaustion   So much of our
predicament is the racket of this life, and by "our predicament"
I think I mean an "our" so much bigger than me and Nate   I refuse

to say "mine and Nate's" or worse "Nate and I" when "me and Nate"
sounds better   One of the confusing things is that, in some sense,
all poetry is noise insofar as it resists the ordinary efficiencies
and practicalities of speaking and writing, in the ways it becomes
a radiant, rather than a delineated, action, and also taps into the currents
of life and death all around us, the things both unsaid
and unsayable   Poetry is a way of listening in, and singing around,
the aspects of living that we ordinarily block out or learn to ignore
as a matter of decorum or administrative necessity   My friend Meg
sent me a surreal tree poem this morning called "Letter from the
    Administrator,"
and it proves her weïrd sister cred once and for all, where the trees are
    office ingénues
pinning up their skirts, unless they're only wearing t-shirts and forgot
their underwear   In that case, they keep their limbs twisting to
    "reap reap reap"
It's creepy and beyond me, so I wouldn't change a thing   Revision is
    the face
of death   The older I get, the more desolate and splintery and sloppy,
    the more
fun I have melting   The more blast site I become   We all sow
    something
Noise and exhaustion seem as meaningful as any, the current undercurrent,
the life force, the deathery, the fog burning off and the birds going crazy,
    the whole
place flooding with fiery white light   The world blowing up in our faces
    feels right

Matt Hart is co-founder and the editor-in-chief of Forklift, Ohio. *He is the author of five books
of poems,* Who's Who Vivid *(Slope Editions, 2006),* Wolf Face *(H_NGM_N Books, 2010),*
Light-Headed *(BlazeVOX, 2011),* Sermons and Lectures Both Blank and Relentless
(Typecast Publishing, 2012), and Debacle Debacle *(H_NGM_N Books, 2013), as well as
several chapbooks. Additionally, his poems, reviews, and essays have appeared in numerous print and
online journals, including* Big Bell, Cincinnati Review, Coldfront, Columbia Poetry Review,
H_NGM_N, Harvard Review, jubilat, Lungfull!, *and* Post Road, *among others. His awards
include a Pushcart Prize, a 2013 individual artist grant from The Shifting Foundation, and fellow-
ships from both the Bread Loaf Writers' Conference and the Warren Wilson College MFA Program
for Writers. He lives in Cincinnati where he teaches at the Art Academy of Cincinnati and plays in
the band* TRAVEL.

Barbara Hamby

All the Buicks in the World

I hate driving. You're a living organism in the middle of another living organism, highways the bloodstream, veins, and arteries that carry belching semis, trucks and SUVs to their terminal orifices. It's hard to imagine North America before the Europeans came with their Protestant love of wide open spaces. A hardwood forest thousands of years old covered the eastern seaboard, old growth oak and pines, ancient as the world itself. None of these trees exist anymore, cut down for dirt farming and roads. Four hundred years ago there were so many birds that a flock could darken the sky for hours as it passed over; hunters didn't have to aim but only raise their muskets, fire, and dinner would come tumbling out of the sky.

I come from a Buick family, which means a Republican family. My grandfather, Clarence Barr, loved Buicks. He would buy a new one every other year. My dad loved Buicks, too. My parents died in a two-year-old 1964 Buick Riviera.

This was the Garden of Eden or at least some form of paradise. In 1600 Shakespeare was writing his plays; in a few years King James would be on the throne, engineering his great translation of the Bible, and birds were so plentiful on the North American continent they could darken the sky at noon. Now the trees were gone, replaced by a super highway system that allows us to zip from New York to Miami in 18 hours with the help of amphetamines and coffee. And the cars—mobile altars on the highway of want. God bless Henry Ford, Walter Chrysler, Louis Chevrolet, and David Dunbar Buick—architects of this brave new world.

I come from a Buick family, which means a Republican family. My grandfather, Clarence Barr, loved Buicks. He would buy a new one every other year. My dad loved Buicks, too. My parents died in a two-year-old 1964

Buick Riviera. My father's sister Dolores had a rich husband, who traded in her Buick every year for a new one. She even bought clothes to match her car. I remember a sky blue convertible, and the cashmere twin set she wore when she and Uncle Raymond pulled up to our house for their annual visit.

A couple of months ago, I was looking for a hammer in my grandmother Emma Barr's garage and found a box of old Buick magazines my grandfather left when he went whereever Baptists go when they die. They call it heaven, but what kind of paradise could it be without dancing and champagne?

Buick—what a word, the alpha and omega. First "Bu-" as in "beautiful; then "-ick" as in "icky." The beauty of whizzing down a highway with your hair blowing and the radio playing "Born to Run"and the ickiness of the grey skies clamped down over Gary, Indiana, like a vise grip. I went to the Barrington, Georgia, Public Library and looked up "buick" in the OED. It's Scottish for "book." And every Buick is a book of the twentieth century: a testament to the open road, a political treatise for a chicken in every pot and a car in every garage, an operating manual for furtive teenaged sex, a ledger of indentured servitude until the note is paid off, a script for cutting down a primeval forest and paving it with asphalt, Long John Silvers, Goofy Golf, and thousands of Texaco and Shell Stations coast-to-coast.

...every Buick is a book of the twentieth century: a testament to the open road, a political treatise for a chicken in every pot and a car in every garage, an operating manual for furtive teenaged sex, a ledger of indentured servitude until the note is paid off...

What I wouldn't give to be able to see that forest, stand at the base of one of those towering oaks, hear the rustle of the canopy far overhead, the birds, animals, and insects we destroyed before we even knew they shared our world. If I believed in God, it would be a god of second chances, a god who would send fools on holy quests to recapture a world that was lost. This would be my quest—to find all the Buicks in the world, to photograph them, draw them, record them in a ledger, detail the detritus of their fenders, transmissions, tail pipes, hoods, trunks, grilles. To find the Buick that was the first car to travel across South

America, driven from Buenos Aires, Argentina, over the Andes to Chile in 1914, to find it in a museum or rusting under a tree in Santiago, the tenement of sixteen squirrels and half a ton of rotting leaves, twigs, seed pods, the love poems of Pablo Neruda, the death warrant of Salvador Allende.

To trek through the dry simooms of Afghanistan to find the Buick Lowell Thomas drove in 1923 for the first expedition in a car to Kabul and Islamabad, search the desert caves, dunes of the jihad, huts of the chador, to discover its tail light being used as a cup, its dashboard as a table, and its hood as the door of a religious school in which the holy Koran is memorized by boys who will never see a woman's ankle or wrist.

To uncover the Buick that in the twenties won a tug-of-war with an elephant, their trunks buried side by side in some African savannah. In 1929, Buick opened a sales office in Shanghai, China. How many Buicks are hidden in the villages of South China, in the high mountains of Tibet's secret mandalas, drowned in the South China Sea during typhoons and monsoons? And what about the war? How is one to locate the blasted shrapnel of tanks and downed planes in WWII that were conceived on the Buick assembly lines in Flint, Michigan. Of the half a million Buicks sold in 1950, where are the corpses and the survivors? Where are the high-compression V-8's, the first torque converter automatic transmission—the Dynaflow—the portholes, the front grilles like the teeth of sharks?

How many years could a pilgrim spend searching for these Buicks, and when they had been gathered up, recorded in the testament of the Lord, could time possibly reverse itself in a momentous creaking of gears and begin to move backwards like a slow, marsupial creature lumbering against the years, stumbling through the trenches of the Somme, wiping the brows of wounded soldiers with Walt Whitman, following the Cherokee nation from Oklahoma back to North Carolina where my

And what about the war? How is one to locate the blasted shrapnel of tanks and downed planes in WWII that were conceived on the Buick assembly lines in Flint, Michigan. Of the half a million Buicks sold in 1950, where are the corpses and the survivors?

father's wild half-breed uncles left the reservation to roam the hills of North Georgia, and to finally wave the white man good-bye as his ships disappeared across the Atlantic, sailing to the Old World with its plagues of smallpox and syphilis. There I would stand with my drops of Indian blood—without mascara, champagne, bikini underwear, blue jeans—in that great forest, the towering oaks and elms, the sky dark with wings.

Barbara Hamby's most recent book of poetry is All-Night Lingo Tango *(Pittsburgh UP, 2009). Her first collection,* Delirium, *was selected by Cynthia McDonald for the Vassar Miller Prize. It also won the Kate Tufts Discovery Prize and the Poetry Society of America's Norma Farber First Book Prize. Her second book,* The Alphabet of Desire, *won the New York University Prize for Poetry and was selected by the New York Public Library as one of the twenty-five best books of 1999. Her third book,* Babel, *was chosen by Stephen Dunn to win the AWP Donald Hall Prize.*

She and her husband, David Kirby, edited an anthology of poetry, Seriously Funny *(Georgia, 2010), a selection of serious poems that are also witty, sly, hilarious, nutty, or crazy funny, and sometimes all of the above.*

She also writes fiction, and her first collection of stories, Lester Higata's 20th Century, *was selected by Paul Harding to win the Iowa Short Fiction/John Simmons Prize. The book was published by the University of Iowa Press in Fall 2010. Her stories have appeared in* TriQuarterly, The Harvard Review, Five Points, The Mississippi Review, Chelsea Review, *and* Shenandoah. *She is Distinguished University Scholar at Florida State University, where she has been teaching for eleven years. She was also a visiting professor at the University of Houston.*

Stephen Dunn

Skulls on Sticks

When I see the righteous coming
my way, sure it's not my way, and two
or three nice vacant ones
step out of their old Chryslers
and knock on my door touting their truths,

I go to my bookshelf and take out
Les Fleurs du Mal and propose
a trade,"My book for your book, even up,"
and insist they'd be getting a bargain.
They always bless me, and I thank them

so they'll turn and go, leave me alone
with my sins, some of which I'd like
to enjoy in private. But often they linger,
as if they might witness something,
and thus be true to their calling.

It's then I tell them the story
about the tribe somewhere in Brazil
that tries to convert the converters,
offers them magic without dogma,
and if that doesn't work just ties them

to a pole in the village center, giving them
the fair choice of death or departure.
Better to let God decide, some missionaries
have been known to say to each other.
The wiser ones put their trust in the fire

already licking their ankles. If still they linger,
murmuring prayers, I add that the natives love
to stir intruders into whatever they're cooking.
Skulls on sticks is one of their specialties.
Their huts are made of bone and gristle.

No Problem

Why do the people who say *no problem*
say *no problem* when you ask
for an extra napkin, or for directions
to the restroom?

If you had entertained a hardship,
you wouldn't have asked,
or would have asked
differently, wouldn't you?

Why can't they say, Sure,
one moment, or, It's over there,
or, I'm sorry, my cockatoo
just died, and I can't speak right now,

forgive me, it will be weeks
before the gloom shall lift
and I'll again be of service.
Why don't they know *no problem*

introduces the notion of problems
when all you wanted
was the simplest of responses.
Would you include me in your will?

May I sleep with your wife?
Which is to say *no problem*
might be fun in certain contexts,
the night suddenly vibrant

with anticipation and angst.
Most likely, though, those who say
no problem won't hear the joke
in the joke, have certain problems

with nuance, use *cool* as a synonym
for yes and anything they like. Want
a milkshake? Cool. Chocolate okay? Cool.
Will you get it for me? No problem—

while the scrupulous are dividing things up,
a yes for this, maybe for that, no way, man,
for the problematical stuff—an effort to sift,
to uplift, be cool, among the impoverishment.

Colloquium

The truth will make you odd,
Flannery O'Connor said,
which made me think it should

have a strange unpleasantness,
like the time my switchblade
seemed to open by itself in the dark.

Truth—T.S. Eliot piped up—
it probably doesn't even exist
without technical accomplishment,

to which V.S. Pritchett added:
Yes, it's all in the art,
you get no credit for living.

I wanted to say something smart
but told the group I had the words
in the wrong order. Give me a second.

Mike Tyson interrupted to say, Most people
don't get no second chances. What's true
is that everyone has a plan until you hit them.

See, it *will* make you odd, I heard
O'Connor insist, who believed awareness
might follow a good slap in the face,

whereupon James Wood countered,
If we're talking literature here, it's only true
if someone gives form to contradiction.

I'm tired of such talk, my ex-wife said
(but not then), I want a variety of many things,
I've had enough of this one thing.

Stephen Dunn is the author of sixteen collections of poetry, including the recent Here and Now *(Norton 2011) and* What Goes On: Selected & New Poems 1995-2009. Different Hours *won the Pulitzer Prize in 2001, and* Loosestrife *was a National Book Critics Circle Award finalist in 1996. His other W.W. Norton books are* New & Selected Poems: 1974-1994, Landscape at the End of the Century, Between Angels, *and* Riffs & Reciprocities: Prose Pairs. *A seventeenth collection* Lines of Defense *is due out from Norton in January 2014.*

Sandra Meek

The Imaginary Heart

To ring pineapple, to fashion canned peach slices into pairs
of parentheses hemming a cottage cheese mound

married to a reef of lettuce—iceberg, rigid enough to endure
without wilting the evening's wait for my father who again

wouldn't be calling and wouldn't be home until evening
had better passed with friends and the ubiquitous bourbon

at the Black Knight bar—this was what my mother
first taught me of salad. Just before she died

she again believed I was her small child so asked
would I survive in this world

if she left and the hospice nurse holding
her other hand assured her

yes, her work was done. Why, before ever
even leaving earth, did the first astronauts script

what they'd say from space? Before they could count
on arriving at orbit visible

only as light, like the luminous lives
enchanting my father sixty years ago on night watch

at ship's aft, all those single-celled animals churned
to a brilliant phosphorescence, though nothing

really was burning. Eighteen, the freedom at last
to sign four years to the sea he'd never

once seen; ashore Oahu, the earth's glittering attic graves lay
beneath him, seedless and expecting

no labor. Childhood's dragging
that larger-than-his-life cotton sack through the fire

of Oklahoma sun distant now
as any apocryphal story of monks twinned

their entire adult lives by shrouds their own faith
stitched to their side. What frees the father

binds the child. For my father's father, arrival
meant that small acreage his own after decades

sharecropping dust; for my father, liaisons that began
while my mother slept in a hospital bed, me safely down

the white hall in a plastic basinet. That chain
of islands, how like studs on a wheel

one sinks beneath the sea as another breaches
its crest of dark stone. What we know

least is what lies directly
beneath our feet: scientists' best hunch—a churning boil

centers what they've circled
and circled from space, photographing to cliché

its blue marble, its clouded eye. At fifteen
with my parents in Vegas I palmed matchbooks

from every casino we visited; at the Riviera,
my father slipped an emptied ashtray into his own

pocket for me as everyone hooted and clapped
for Bobby Vinton cutting off "Sealed With a Kiss" to french

some woman in the audience. Not to find a single
dark-haired young girl on the beach

sailors could pay to take
their picture with, waxy cups of plumeria

pierced and strung to leis evidencing whatever story they might
be weaving for home: that surprised him

most, returning late in his seventies to show
his aging daughters his own lost youth: as if those islands

long stitched to a single star in the flag he served
might have lived on as perpetual fantasy, festive

as the Rainbow Bomb Parties held the year I was born,
all-night viewers on Honolulu rooftops celebrating

with specially concocted cocktails—Atomic Fizz, Rocket Romp,
     The Van Allen
Belt of Bourbon—the last named for Defense's

latest craze, what Operation Starfish Prime's atomic explosion
was to bend that night, charging the sky to how many brilliant never-

before-seen colors, because discovery meant something
else to blow up, and that Pacific sky tonight could tomorrow

be Moscow's streets or our own bomb-shelterless
neighborhood where my mother would long hold us to a tableau

of Mother and Daughters Dutifully Waiting before a chilling
slab of meat and little plates of salad as if that

could make up A Happy Family whether or not my father
returned home before midnight. Because my parents never

should have married, they did so twice. A woman's work
is never done. Misery made up

how much of that closed-in house's cloud
nine months thickening the long

Colorado winter before the windows could finally
be flung open? But every

one of us smoked then. And if it's true that what's held too tightly
tumors the body, what pearled her lungs

like tiny river stones, holding her beneath the water rising
through her own scarred chest, was it anger she couldn't outlive

to share this fresh pineapple my father, now advancing
in his own cancer, has had fresh-flown in

for my sister and me, as much memento of the trip we three took together
as fruit of the one time he'd signed on to something

he'd never once regretted. That perfect reconciliation
of sweetness and light glowing

before us, his open-armed gesture
towards the table said what she

never could: There is no return
to a world without fire. Girls, go ahead.

Eat.

Protea lepidocarpodendron
(Black-Bearded Protea)

Silvermine Nature Reserve, Western Cape, South Africa

Each outsized bloom's a cup on the cusp
of inflorescence, flowers

held at bay: half fist, half swan's
folded wing, each a downy clutch

of quills dampered by cream bracts
tipped a burgundy-black tattooing

fading as my father's did from
recognition—18, shore-leave drunk, goading

shipmates, still he chose the smallest in the book
of offerings, what best to shrink

away from: his bicep mucked a flowering
he couldn't name. To define

that day's place is to again dissolve
in fog so thick its milky smoke

stains, breathing in; even my hands
clouded with descent that robbed

all direction but the bite of jagged cliffs
knived over sea, trail a question

I failed to answer to until late
afternoon's clearing threaded me back

to a now abandoned lot, everything
missing where I'd

stupidly stashed it: car lock
you cracked, tires you slashed I

drove to the rims, that metallic rattle on gravel
the tin can-clatter ghost tailing me

of the day I cast off my own name
just to slip free of my father's.

In its first painting, only the bloom's
complete, that single specimen

Bauer, at eighteenth century's end, detailed
down to the beaked

outer bracts, leaves and stem left a faintly
penciled gray. Unfinished

as what I've failed
to picture beyond descending mist

steeled in a bivalve of silver light, my purse's
compact mirror: your face,

your appraising eye I
can't catch as you sort camera

from lip balm, passport from lunch sack
you've eaten my peanut butter

sandwich from even before you test the flashlight's
narrow beam, twisting its blue fashioned best

to betray blood's spattered trail to the night-
vision red pitched to illumine

charts that constellate what's missing
from Cape Town's drained sky, what sundown disappears

with the flats you came up from—tin houses bogged
beyond the bright city grid that bleeds

even your unelectrified sky blank
as my pocket notebook you stack with the packet

of tissues, nail file, hairbrush: play,
I imagine, for your youngest.

Truth? Even my photographs fog as much as flower
what I sought that day, what Linnaeus christened

to preserve his own good name, hedging
uncertainty, species he knew solely through his period's

penchant for florilegia, not by the dissection
of his own touch. Elusive he clouded

allusive: Protea for Proteus, for that mythic
shape-shifting, not

for knowledge, future that men kept holding
him down to. To be no one

in a country that doesn't care to know you
is one version of home. Out of range

but for one quartered second's
connection, a single text lit the cell

I held exploratory, morphed
aggressive, stomach liver bone brain

Dad—message I must only have read
as fragments, as crouched against

the road's view, you must have been deep
in your own best work just then: crowbar,

knife in hand. That undocumented
night, as I braided my hair back in tangle

for the photographs that would restore me
to name and place, as I watched

from my hotel window two friendly battleships
nose into False Bay, the harbor sundowning

to a shimmer of refracted light that would spill
the dusk streets with crew-cut boys razored

toward the end days of youth, did you
picture me? Did you see

them, Protea lepidocarpodendron, that rare stand
only lost I finally found—bush

after bush, every flower head's pearly grail
inked to what survives the poverty

of night's slow burn: near exhausted coals
rinsed in morning to rescue what still

might warm, the crumbling black bits
at the heart. Was it you who patted them

into cakes, soft fists mapped to the tracks
in your palms a day's winter sun

would harden? So tenuous the hold
of some Proteas, to dig the foundation

for a single house could erase them forever
from this earth. But the face you stole

was paper, not bone, and whatever limit
stamped my book, my father's urging stay

left me to witness what I'd crossed
a world for, what I barely saw

though all I did for weeks was look:
that spectacle, spring. In one gold-

shrouded view, desiccation
and bloom; desert dunes morphed

to meadows, Namaqualand daisies' fringed wheels
and succulents I could distinguish

only by scale: some larger than my outstretched hand,
some less than the tip of my thumb, as if

what had shifted was only the matter
of perspective, as white sand deepened

to red fields at dusk—shattered stone starred
by innumerable black eyes lashed electric

white, neon blue, magenta bright as the King
Protea, your nation's flower

rayed across every rand in that roll surely
you pocketed first.

Truth? I made it back
for goodbye, and what I can't let go

is what I can't know:
how what's held
so long as seed can suddenly
riot into bloom; how what's stared directly down

still eludes. And that second charge to the Cape Town
McDonald's, the last to blink through

before my card cancelled: who you went back for
to feed, your confederates, or

your children. But truth's what we tell
when no one's listening, and lacking

more than the most rudimentary vocabulary
for anatomy, or grace, hunger's all

I'm holding you to: brain, heart, bone.

Sandra Meek is the author of four books of poems, Road Scatter *(Persea Books, 2012),* Biogeography, *winner of the Dorset Prize (Tupelo Press, 2008),* Burn *(2005), and* Nomadic Foundations *(2002), as well as a chapbook,* The Circumference of Arrival *(2001). She is also the editor of an anthology,* Deep Travel: Contemporary American Poets Abroad *(Ninebark 2007), which was awarded a 2008 Independent Publisher Book Award Gold Medal. A recipient of a 2011 National Endowment for the Arts Fellowship in Poetry, she has twice been awarded Georgia Author of the Year, in 2006 for* Burn, *and in 2003 for* Nomadic Foundations, *which also was awarded the Peace Corps Writers Award in Poetry. She is a co-founding editor of Ninebark Press, director of the Georgia Poetry Circuit, poetry editor of the Phi Kappa Phi Forum, and Dana Professor of English, Rhetoric, and Writing at Berry College in Georgia, USA.*

Dan Albergotti

Splinter & Sneeze

When I would get a splinter as a child,
my father would strike a match and then hold
one of my mother's thin sewing needles
in the flame until it glowed a bright red,
sanitizing the steel. Then he'd hold me
down and dig into my flesh to retrieve
the shard of wood. When I think of him now,
that's the sweetest image I can recall,
the concentration on his face as he
stabbed at his child's finger or foot, as he
tried to make something right by digging out
what's wrong.   He used to sneeze in sets of three—
two quick bursts and then a dramatic pause
building suspense before the crescendo
of an enormous third. My sister coughed
the scornful laugh she'd learned from him, mocking
his involuntary functions, the things
he couldn't control, just as he mocked her.
She'd shake her head from side to side and snort.

I had a professor once who told me
that his great-grandfather, a foot soldier
in the Confederate army, survived
three days of hell at Gettysburg and then
came home after the war, got a splinter
in his hand, developed an infection,
and died. Life before antibiotics
was like that: every day a chance to die.

But I guess that applies to any time.

I had another professor who taught
the psychology of aging, a field
that assumes normal life expectancy.
I learned about natural human response
to weakening health, fading memory,
the inevitability of death.
All the things we expect to come on slow.
He returned home for part of the summer
one year to visit his aging parents.
One July morning he went for a jog
around the neighborhood where he'd grown up,
and a woman driving down the same road
sneezed, sneezed so hard that her body shook, sneezed
so hard that she lost control of her car,
and swerved, just briefly, onto the shoulder.
My professor lay there a little while
and then was nowhere at all anymore.

In ancient Greece, sneezes were thought to be
prophetic signs from the gods—good omens,
usually. When a foot soldier answered
the end of Xenophon's speech with a sneeze,
his comrades heard it as a divine cheer,
the gods' guidance to their deliverance.
By the Middle Ages, Europeans
had grown a bit more skeptical, fearing
the sneeze as a potentially fatal
expulsion of the life force. *God bless you,*
they said, thinking divine intervention
would be needed to spare the sneezer's life.

Maybe one of Xenophon's foot soldiers
managed to make it home after the wars
and caught his own death splinter in a thumb
or sneezed himself into oblivion.

Maybe my sister's life could have been good,
happy, if she'd gotten more oxygen
at birth, if her brain hadn't been damaged.
Or if the damage had been great enough
to keep her from understanding her life
too well. Maybe we could have been happy.

The world and time and every life are grand
and very, very small.

                  And sometimes poems
are very, very small, but feel as if
they could do anything. Sometimes I wish
I could turn time backward and say just once
God bless you to my father and mean it.
Go back and tell my mother *I'm sorry*.
Go back to thirteen years before my birth,
to a delivery room, and try to help
untangle a cord. Go back to somewhere
where I'm not, take a needle to this life,
and work at mending, or at digging out.

Ghazal: The Prelude

Sometimes even endings feel like prelude.
Every postscript could be titled "Prelude."

You have to wonder about Wordsworth's plan
if he titled fourteen books *The Prelude.*

After he gave up novels, Hardy wrote
his best poems, all the prose merely prelude.

So many unfinished projects: Chaucer,
Byron, Keats. What's left is only prelude.

James Dickey said we're all just amateurs,
here too briefly to move beyond prelude.

I hesitate to begin even as
my time slips by, erased before prelude.

Tell me. What thoughts are worth words, worth writing
when each dangling line feels like mere prelude?

Dan Albergotti is the author of The Boatloads *(BOA Editions, 2008), selected by Edward Hirsch as the winner of the 2007 A. Poulin, Jr. Poetry Prize, and a limited-edition chapbook,* The Use of the World *(Unicorn Press, 2013). A new full-length collection,* Millennial Teeth, *won the Crab Orchard Series Open Competition in 2013 and will be published by Southern Illinois University Press in 2014. Albergotti's poems have appeared in* The Cincinnati Review, Five Points, The Southern Review, The Virginia Quarterly Review, *and Pushcart Prize XXXIII, as well as other journals and anthologies. A graduate of the MFA program at UNC Greensboro and former poetry editor of* The Greensboro Review, *he is an associate professor at Coastal Carolina University, where he teaches literature and writing courses and edits* Waccamaw.

Bob Hicok

The big game

The quarterback kept throwing touchdowns
to waiters and caddies
into his eighties—it was a habit
bred of high school and everyone loved
spiking the ball, loved unfurling
the touchdown dance they'd worked on
without knowing it in that place
in the brain that hides
from the brain—then he died
and the whole town came to his funeral
with footballs and pompons
and fucked under the bleachers
and rolled joints
fatter than reggae, fatter than birdsong
waking the day—you see why soccer
will never take over—this need
to go long—to run a fly—an out—
a hitch and go—that's all
this has been—one hitch and go
after another—hit me—I'm open—
I keep saying that—I keep meaning
to mean that—I keep meaning
to touch the cheerleader
with a smile that's a true friend
to joy

New neighbors

The farmer's honest:
the river gave me some of your land, he tells the woman
who bought the farm that sleeps beside his, standing there
with two fists of mud, an accounting of the storm.
I imagine that's a guess on your part, she says,
and he replies yes, a guess, like how many stars
there are is a guess a person makes or a computer
when we should be asking the sky. What about the rain
that falls on my land but licks its way onto yours,
or the shadows of my apple trees, or the wind
that touches how I smell in the morning and rolls
that discovery to you? He thinks about the true scale
of his debt by turning his head to the left,
where unbeknownst to anyone, there's crack in the air
only he can see, almost a mouth, nearly a door
in or out, he can never decide. When he turns back
he has an answer, he does owe her for all those things,
and for singing at dusk, for the sound of her voice
running away from home. This last thing's
a revelation, I didn't know I've been singing,
she tells him, and turns her head to the right,
where unbeknownst to anyone, there's a feeling
of a bell she can almost ring, hovering out of reach
of being real. That's where I stand to listen to you,
he adds, pointing where an oak held court
until he was ten, a spot where one night, lightning
wanted to be and got its way as I watched, a sound
like all the birds there have ever been
or could ever be taking off at once, he tells her,
and worries that in telling the truth
in this simple way, he has lied.

First a fort, then a city, now an island

My friend Bill Fuchs has been killing
stray dogs who roam in snarling packs,
for safety at first but recently to eat.
Bill Fuchs loves dogs but Bill Fuchs
loves eating more than dying and once
Detroit goes bankrupt, its credit rating
will be so bad it won't be able to buy
a car. This will earn Detroit
The Irony of the Year Award. Since I
was a kid, I've loved Detroit
as a garden where factories
were born and died and Tiger Stadium
smelled like linseed oil, hot dogs
and piss. To continue loving
Bill Fuchs and Detroit, I've had to accept
that Bill Fuchs, on any given day,
has some shepherd or sheepdog
in him and that these offers
of life are given and rescinded
every second without concern
for the appearance of need. Detroit
can't leave Detroit and Bill Fuchs
can't leave his breath and when I visit
his crapfest of a home, I wipe my feet
at the door and ignore the rifle
in the corner, sure in another life
or year, it'll be mine.

Sometimes I feel the universe is in good hands

Shhhh—I haven't read Moby Dick. I tried
to check the water-damaged edition out of the library
for the irony but wasn't allowed to. The tan copy
is uglier but less drowned, I ran into a former student
as I carried it across campus, she showed me
where she'd torn out a page to roll a joint & smoke
the White Whale to help her write a paper
about the symbolism of the sea with the munchies.
Since last I'd seen her, her hair had turned
robin's egg blue and spiky, like if you tried to touch
the buried treasure of her mind and were a balloon, ouch
or as a warning to passing clouds to keep their distance,
I am not an interpreter of hair gel or a naturalist
but when I told her she reminded me of a sea urchin,
she smiled. While she'll never be a model,
there are whole fields of twiggy beauty waiting
to be harvested for television, she has the rarer kind
of nuclear energy the country needs in her smile
and her curiosity yesterday about how a less precise
system of measurement leads to a more exact way
of determining how far stars are from the comfy bed
all matter shared at the start. Beats me, I said,
wondering too how the stick became the ruler
and the ruler the micrometer and the micrometer
the laser, only because I had stopped to love
the adventure of her head and be changed.

The gondola I'd been building was almost done—it just
needed some basil in the garden of my ear
to save space—some sun in the sky of my wife's eyes
to spare us the vagaries of weather—in a week
or two we'd be far away under a thought balloon—
but while trying to convince our horse she couldn't bring
her horse, I realized how hypocritical that was—and
of course our horse's horse wanted to bring her horse—
I had gone around for years saying everyone should have
a horse and now was paying for my glibness—in bars,
while making love, even burning down the meth lab next door
I would say that—now there's no end to the horses
who get to come along wherever we go—aren't we lucky—
isn't this life intent on being a miracle—clearly
the skill you should learn—the one that never
goes out of style—tying a bow on a box—a box
you'll hand to someone you love—a box dressed
in its red or green or yellow bow—a big box—
an empty box—to make room for everything

"Bob Hicok's poetry is a...temporary solace from the chaos of the world," declares the LA Times. Words
for Empty and Words for Full *(University of Pittsburgh Press, 2010) is his most recent collection.*
This Clumsy Living *was awarded the Bobbitt Prize from the Library of Congress,* Animal Soul *was
a finalist for the National Book Critics Circle Award, and* The Legend of Light *received the Felix
Pollak Prize in Poetry and was named a 1997 ALA Booklist Notable Book of the Year. Other titles
are* Insomnia Diary *(Pitt, 2004), and* Plus Shipping *(BOA, 1998). Hicok is an associate professor
of English at Virginia Tech. Prior to teaching, Hicok worked for nearly two decades as an automotive
die designer and eventually owned his own business.*

Cotton Candy. 20x18. Oil on Panel. 2012.
Charles Keiger.

Picnic. 16x18. Oil on panel. 2012.
Charles Keiger.

Fish Tale. 16x18. Oil on panel. 2012.
Charles Keiger.

The Rehearsal. 16x13.5. Oil on panel. 2012.
Charles Keiger.

The Sky is Falling. 16x14. Oil on panel. 2010.
Charles Keiger.

The Optimist II. 14x12. Oil on panel. 2010.
Charles Keiger.

Bermuda Triangle. 14x12. Oil on panel. 2012.
Charles Keiger.

Dogwood. 16x14. Oil on panel. 2007.
Charles Keiger.

The Woodcarver. 24x22. Oil on wood. 2013.
Charles Keiger.

Arrival of Fun. 12x14. Oil on panel. 2012.
Charles Keiger.

Kevin Boyle

The Compromise Candidate

Because of the rifts and personalities, the loathing and envy,
Though we all agreed to shift from centigrade to Celsius

In honor of Celsius who placed water's boiling point at 0
And marked its freezing point at 100, we could not agree

On the symbol for Celsius, with some holdouts advocating
For °C, in honor of the c in *cento*, a nod towards Rome's Latin,

And others, the Northerners mainly, preferring an homage
To the Swede Celsius, and so they rallied behind the sign °C.

As a Catholic who had been to Rome and spoken Latin in its streets,
I preferred °C a hundred times over the Swedish °C,

But I had also once loved a Swede named Catarina, who blew
Both hot and cold, she of the fiery ice, and so on non-feast days

I found myself in the opposing camp, arguing with those
In my own think tank, wanting to resurrect certain devilish moves,

Suggesting we gut and flay my closest comrades, my erstwhiles.
After the voting and re-voting on the table's shape and the multi-modal

Modes allowed, as winter gave way to spring's mud,
We all sensed a thaw, the forsythias speaking first, followed by

The crocus family, the tulips pleading from their corms,
And then a whole hedge of rhododendrons spoke with a loud voice

About compromise and making kin from kith, and so, though
I still have sleepless nights, sometimes regretting my vote,

Sometimes drawing a blade on the moon's shadows, we found
Common ground, only burying the hatchet in each other's necks

In our dreams, and came to accept as a body the compromise
Candidate, °C, that had been launched as a trial balloon

That seemed to have traction, then legs, until finally it was assumed
Into the heavens and we could see eye to eye as it rose like an open hand.

Drunk Excuse

He was driving home at night, late at night, from the beach—*beach or shore?*—and he was tired—*acid or drink?*—and he just kept driving, a lot of pine trees and not much else—*finish up please, it's time*—when he ran over something—*his homework?*—and he thought maybe it was a deer, and his buddy—he was with someone else—*his lover? Make it interesting*—maybe his lover, maybe his friend from childhood, and the buddy thinks maybe it's a bear—*come on, plausibility, reasonable doubt*—and they decide to stop—*big fucking mistake, drive on, she said, drive on*—maybe it's somebody's dog, so they back up and the driver sees in the mirror in the white lights a body, and thinks it's a woman—*his girlfriend who raised bears?*—and he begins to freak out, and his buddy says, Let's get out of here—*Drive on, she said*—but the driver stops the car and comes out—*Comes out of the closet, you mean*—with a stick in his hand—*What stick?*—just in case it's alive and an animal, but it's dead, he can see that now, and a woman—he turns her over with his boot, gently—*kicks her in the cunt, as Beckett would say*—and begins to cry—*What, it's his momma?*—and bends down to look into her face that hasn't been crushed, the stomach and legs are crushed, she's been run over multiple times, and he puts his lips to her lips, thinking maybe he can save her, but there's nothing there, and he feels so devastated, so ruined, he collapses in his buddy's arms—*What did I tell*—and the two of them make a pact to tell no one, this is their secret, then the driver reaches for his phone and calls the cops to turn himself in or call for help or speak to someone not there or submit to questioning, that back and forth, give and take, keeping himself occupied before the long depression takes hold again.

Northern Wind

While holding a canapé and an empty fluted glass
At the cocktail party I was asked about my walk of life,
I fired back a question about her dress size, and pointed
To my shoes—this is my walk of life! Mildly untied
New Balance cross-trainers and I dabble in the market,
Mainly start-ups but also veteran performers, perhaps
Like yourself? I'm a gastropod aficionado, she said,
I market what I harvest at high-end farmer's markets,
And I minister to those in want. Do you want to slip
Into something more comfortable than this air, one of us
Said, gossiping as if the phyllo dough had suddenly risen
From its grave inside our throats. A black-tie trio
Grasped at straws with their mouths while they bowed
Their strings. I suddenly decided to play name
Your allergy, and we spent a good chunk of the evening
Recalling allergies we hadn't remembered for years,
Band-aid glue, wheat-free gluten, peanuts and harvest moons.
When we spoke of our spouses what a surprise it was
To hear they each shared a birthday in June, early
To mid June. Suddenly I saw the plate-glass field
Astride the lab held a doe and two little ones, all tawny.
You hunt, I asked. You bet, she said, then showed
How her breast had been removed in order to allow
The bow to be drawn back in one fluid motion.
Like the Amazons? You bet, she said, then showed
How she'd let fly, a mime of archer, bow and arrow
With fletches made of hen feathers. I feel unfaithful
Just speaking with you, let's date surreptitiously.
Alcohol makes me want to violate rigid social norms

With you. You are such a sweetheart, she said,
But I just bought a new app and want to learn its features,
But here's my card, let me know when you're in
The town next to this one, which is my hometown.
I am seeing a new acupuncturist I want you to meet,
And with that she turned to someone else, the slit
In her dress dehiscing as she stepped away. Christ,
I felt both forlorn and kind of weird, a small rain
Coming down on the far field where the deer once roamed.

Kevin Boyle's book, A Home for Wayward Girls, *was published by New Issues and his chapbook,* The Lullaby of History, *won the Mary Belle Campbell Poetry Prize. His poems have appeared in* Alaska Quarterly, Hollins Critic, North American Review, Northwest Review, Pleiades, Poetry East *and* Virginia Quarterly Review. *He has degrees from the University of Pennsylvania, Boston University and the University of Iowa's Writers' Workshop. Originally from Philadelphia, Kevin teaches at Elon University in North Carolina.*

Kristofer Whited

The Forgiveness of Animals

Clemency Parker had lived in the valley outside of Fresno, California for thirty of his fifty years; he didn't farm or raise livestock like his neighbors, though, which was always a source of shame for his wife.

Carol Parker was a short, plump woman who dressed in flower-printed polyester clothes and kept a small mauve bible in the drawer of her vanity. Inside the back cover, she maintained a record of every time Clemency had disappointed her. Beginning, of course, with her most apparent let-down: April 3, 1977—*bought wrong house (wasted insurance money)*. Over the next three decades, she developed a system of dealing with his failures: she'd pull away from him, eyes to the floor, and retreat down the long, narrow hallway to their bedroom. Carol made no qualms about her record keeping; she did not hide it. He would eventually follow her into the bedroom, stand opposite in the room, glimpsing her in the mirror of her station. When she was done scribbling, she would spend the next hour silently flipping and reading. Clemency could only assume she was looking for passages relevant to her present sacrifice—that particular brand of forgiveness the circumstances required.

These are some listings that Clemency had glanced at: October 11, 1980—*didn't take job in Sacramento (three more dollars an hour)*; January 30, 1982—*left car windows down in rainstorm (asleep on the couch)*; November 6, 1984—*wasted vote on Walter Mondale*; July 4, 1988—*turned Jerry Wilkins down on cattle-deal (better life)*; March 10, 1990—*picked wrong restaurant (Anniversary)*;

May 1, 1992—*won't raise chickens (food)*; May 2, 1992—*won't raise goats (milk/lawncare)*.

At work, in the nearby city of a half million, Clemency was the cut-man on a crew of carpenters. He kept his saw immaculately clean, two new blades behind the seat of his small pick-up—at his own expense—just in case he couldn't find one in the job trailer when he needed it. The Swiss, the boss had said, couldn't design a better cut-man. Because he was meticulous and efficient, a method tested and tenured by practice and time. He wore a straw hat, and a red bandana tied around his neck to collect the sweat that flowed from his once scraggly beard. Clemency had begun growing it a month into the job. Thirty years he'd watched it thicken and turn gray in spots, hunkered over the raw materials of a home built for folks he didn't know, but who deserved his best nonetheless.

The boys would holler measurements from the second story, or drop scrap pieces of lumber with lists of desired lengths for the top-plate. But he truly enjoyed the days he cut in the roof—the rafters. A thirty-two degree bevel down the long run of a 9/12 pitch never failed to test him and to engage him, even after so many years. He thought himself a sculptor in those moments, rigging the raw materials with the spaces to fit their purpose, seeing the rafter in the twelve foot length of 2x10 from the moment it hit his saw horses. He wasn't making angles; he was finding them, employing them. For Clemency Parker, there was no doubt: those rafters already existed. And by the time he got the second 2x10 up and ready, the first sent to its destination on the back of whatever greenhorn was humping for the crew that summer, Clemency would hear the boys shout from around the back wall.

"Jesus, Clem," one would yell, "I just sent you them numbers. You didn't even give me time to smoke a fucking cigarette!"

Then, with a secret grin, as he began sculpting again, he imagined those boys laying the rafter down—open faced against the ridgeboard, the beveled long run resting snugly across the plywood of the valley. Then it would come: affirmation, from the fans of his art.

"Fits like a Sunday dress in L.A., Clem!"

After work, the hour drive home, from city to orchards to hills, always gave Clemency just the right amount of time to unwind, to straighten his back in the seat, tighten his muscles, and feel the day's work in the pleasant shooting energy from the back of his skull to the knuckles of his toes. The air always cooled just before the Visalia turnoff, the valley just beyond that. Their ten acres sat atop an exposed hump of foothill, steep declines on all sides—*un*farmable, to Carol's distaste. But it allowed a regal view of the flat valley one hundred-fifty feet below, scattered groves of grappling oaks, pastoral spreads of annual grasses, and the fencelines that sectioned it all.

One evening in early October, he cleared a few branches and leaves from the small concrete patio, surmised his valley, and took a breath before entering the door. He got inside and peeled the boots from his feet.

"Jerry Wilkins called," Carol said.

She sat at the small desk on the opposite side of the large, open living room, tapping a pencil on a pad of paper.

"Oh, I had a very good day. And how are you, dear?"

"Ha ha. He was going up hunting this weekend, and he wanted to know if you'd go."

"Hunting? For what? " Clemency unbuttoned his light flannel. "Deer, probably."

"*For what*. I don't know. You're a man, what do *men* hunt?"

Clemency looked across the floor then up to his wife, tracing the trail of the sting she'd just delivered, as if her words had all the iridescence of a greasy slug. The mauve bible lay behind her elbow near the pad of paper. *On-deck*, he thought. She no longer faced him. She'd turned, and was righting herself in the swivel chair. He looked at the plastic clothes and sensible shoes, thought about what she'd just said, and lamented secretly about the day they'd met.

Clemency looked across the floor then up to his wife, tracing the trail of the sting she'd just delivered, as if her words had all the iridescence of a greasy slug.

It was on a Greyhound heading east across the Central Valley in May of 1976. Clemency was stumbling back from San Francisco with a thin face and dilated pupils and eight thousand dollars spent of the lump sum he was given upon his parents' deaths. Carol had been in a denim dress with bib overall straps and a white tee, returning from a week-long bible study in some countryside around the Bay area. He was shocked when she crossed the aisle and plopped next to him. She asked if everything was all right. His mind was reeling, and he struggled to speak. "I lost it," he kept repeating. "I lost it."

"What honey," she asked, "what'd you lose?"

"I lost my bible in San Francisco."

She laughed. "A lot of people do," she said. She asked where he was headed.

"Home," he answered.

"Where's home?"

"Indiana," he told her. She asked what he did, *what was his work?* He thought about the question and fell silent for several minutes until he spun back to her and finally answered, *carpenter.*

"Well, my father knows a contractor in Fresno," she'd said, and she took his hand. "You made it all the way out here for a reason, didn't you?"

He looked at that woman now, his wife, sitting in their living room. The bitterness behind her eyes, the discomfort in her shoulders, the displeasure she took in returning his gaze and speaking to him. This was his life, decades in the making. When did it all start working against him? When had his life gone from something he created to something he feared and pitied and needed to forgive on a daily basis? He turned and pushed open the bifold door of the bathroom by the back door and went in to piss. He stared at the faux-wood *Bless this Mess* plaque above the toilet. It was her parents' divorce. That's when *she*'d changed at least, and the record keeping began.

Clemency and Carol would find out, a year into their own marriage, that the contractor her father knew happened also to be her mother's lover. Until then, Carol had questioned her father's politics, and the way they were intertwined with his stern faith. There were several tense dinners and outings during which she'd argued with him. Clemency had figured, in fact, that that had been the reason she'd taken him on—in the raggedy shape he was in at their meeting—so willingly. Proving something to Daddy. In that first year, she'd even commented that her father's *preachings* echoed many of the fundamentalists the bible—in her reading then—told her to watch out for. "She actually said that!" Clemency announced to the plaque in a hoarse whisper. He flushed the toilet and ran the water and washed his hands. When the affair was discovered and her mother's love for the contractor professed, her father was left broken, and his faith pressed against its seams like a bloated corpse. So Carol seemed to clasp onto that faith, as ridiculous and unfounded as it was, as if to defend it against the unreasonableness, and obvious transgression, of her mother's betrayal. Day by month, month by year, that unreasonable stern faith became her own.

He came out of the bathroom, went to the refrigerator, and grabbed a beer. Cracked it, and flipped the cap into the trashcan.

"Cause I was thinking," Carol began again.

"You were?"

"This goes well, Jerry might invite you with him and his friends more often. And the money you make working all the time wouldn't buy the meat you could take off a couple deer a year."

"I could just start hunting myself."

She didn't hide her chuckle.

"You know, hunting means *killing* things, Clemency. You going to go from zero to a hundred just like that, all by yourself?" She pushed the pad of paper out of the way. "Jerry's been doing it a while. You'd do better with him."

Clemency could almost *feel* her inching toward that mauve bible, and he dropped a thirsty swig down his throat and wiped his lips.

"I didn't realize the deer admire Jerry as much as everybody else does."

"What's that supposed to—"

"Don't," Clemency said.

"Well? Are you going to pass up *another* opportunity for Jerry to help us?"

And just like that, Independence Day of 1988 was right there in his mind's eye. The conjuring of such humiliations had become his wife's most proficient talent.

Clemency and Carol had joined others in an annual tradition at Jerry's house on Jerry's farm. Jerry Wilkins bought the flat, pastured thirty-acre parcel that Clemency had opted against when he and Carol first came to the valley. Jerry had flourished from eight head of cattle. The host made an announcement over beef ribs that he would be willing to include all his invited guests in his latest, greatest cattle-deal, one accounting for five hundred head on eight-hundred acres north of Pine Flat Creek.

Clemency cringed at the thought of how much money his neighbor was talking about.

"Jerry knows what he's talking about," Carol insisted, moving her fingers to Clemency's arm and squeezing.

Later, Jerry sauntered up and asked Carol and Clemency and the others to join him. His eyes were glassy and round, his black cowboy hat pushed past his forehead, his breath reeking of cheap beer. He led them to his barn. The beef was strapped by canvas belt, one raising the rear five feet in the air, one securing the shoulders. The beef's neck and jaw tightened in a belted noose hung from a four by four slung through the trusses. Wilkins stood to it, and brought the knife across clean like a showman, giving Carol a quick wink as he stepped away. The blood poured out and the beef's eyes rolled for a second then the left one fell dead on Clemency. They were walking food, he tried to remind himself, these cows, it's good to bleed the meat. Carol had a look of victory on her face. Wilkins wiped the blade on his Levis. And a baffling, spontaneous applause arose from the barn's other attendants.

At first, the eye was brown at its center with a band of primary yellow circling it. But as Clemency watched it all fade to brown, then black, the cow's legs shuddering, its nostrils exhaling blood, he felt the pressure in his chest. It welled in his throat and solidified behind his eyes, pushing for release. But not now, he thought. Not here in front of Wilkins and his friends, not in front of Carol. Not in the presence of this dying steer. The blood had pooled beneath the beast's muscular chest, his hooves frantically dancing in it like a crazed soldier. The hot afternoon breeze swept through from the vent near the ceiling on the north wall. Clemency gasped and buried his nose and mouth into his flannelled elbow. When the beef went to one knee, when most of its weight now hung in the taut noose, when the blackened eye popped from its socket and dangled from a curling red tendon, Clemency winced and held his stomach—as a distraction from his eyes—and bolted for the door.

"So you want to go, or not?" Carol said, still tapping her pencil. "I'm sure he won't wait forever for an answer."

Here he was again. He was angry. He was disappointed that this woman—his wife—still preferred her hopeful version of him to the man he actually was.

"Sure, why not," Clemency said, suddenly resolved, taking more than a little pleasure in the unexpectedness of his answer.

He watched his wife. She could hardly conceal her pleasure, straightening herself in her chair.

"Really? Cause I was thinking. The money you'd make working this weekend couldn't buy the meat you could take off a deer."

"You said that."

He moved to the sink and rinsed his face in cold water, clearing the gathered sawdust from his eyes with the tips of calloused fingers. Drying off with the towel—without want or warning—he thought of his aunt, Cheryl. So, of course, he thought of Uncle Burt.

In the spring of 1974, on a slow, thoughtful walk through the small garden behind the First Methodist Church in Mossberg, Indiana, Burt Whitaker and Pastor Duane Gooden decided that it was an injustice to have the front double-doors, on an otherwise fine house of God, in such disrepair. An insult, they were, to the upstanding and faithful congregation, who had, in the weeks previous, been relegated to a side entrance. Burt, a local small-time contractor and carpenter, offered his services as well as the services of his seventeen-year-old nephew. The new doors themselves, the two men decided, would be a donation that Pastor Gooden insisted he would consider for the next several weeks when the plate was passed around. All of this, Burt told Clemency on their ride home that afternoon. Clemency, not surprised that he was not consulted, agreed with silence that it was the right thing to do.

Two months earlier, Clemency had been sent to live with his Aunt Cheryl, his mother's only sibling, and her husband, Burt, after his parents were killed in a car accident coming home from dinner up north. His father had had a few glasses of wine after dessert and simply lost control on a tight corner, breaking the Ford truck nearly in two on a telephone pole. "If it's any consolation, son," Sheriff Jenkins, a friend of the family, had said, "it don't look like they suffered." It wasn't. But Clemency did not cry. He told the Sheriff he'd be a minute and took a look around the living room: his father's slippers next to the La-Z-Boy and Kesey novel laying open on the arm, his mother's knitting material bundled in an unfinished sweater on the floor next to her spot on the sofa, her stack of *Mother Earth News* close. He went to his room and packed a small bag of his things and left the tiny house his parents had been renting while saving to build a home of their own.

It was with Burt and Cheryl that Clemency had begun attending church. His parents, though spiritual people, didn't subscribe to church being a necessary demonstration of faith. This had always been a matter of dissatisfaction to Cheryl, one she insisted on reiterating to a mourning Clemency in the weeks following her sister's untimely death. Usually at dinner, just after grace.

"That was a God-fearing woman, from a God-fearing family until that man came along."

"Now, Cheryl, quit," Burt would insist, motioning in Clemency's direction. "Have some respect."

Clemency would hang his head from his place at their table, trying to swallow and keep down the chicken and potatoes that should have tasted good, potatoes that should have tasted like his mother's.

A week after Burt and Pastor Gooden had reached their agreement, as the other parishioners were shaking hands and waving goodbye and heading home, Cheryl long gone, Clemency and Burt changed clothes, pulled the tools from the bed of Burt's truck, and began removing the weathered birch trim from the ailing doors.

Clemency watched his uncle. He was immediately impressed with Burt's ethic, his method, his little tricks to deal with the troubles he encountered: using a chunk of wood under his hammer to increase leverage while pulling a stubborn nail; spinning an eight penny nail in his fingers and striking its tip with his hammer just once, dulling it, to prevent the wood from splitting when he sank it; applying a thumbfull of spit across a small, stray hammer indention on the new trim to force the wood to swell, erasing the unsightly mark. Clemency was smiling for the first time in a while. These were laws of nature. Burt wasn't making solutions, the solutions were already there.

Pastor Gooden sauntered out of his community-bought house and across the gravel lot to where they were working.

"You know, I appreciate this, fellas," he said, wiping his brow with his forearm, "but I'd rather not have you toil on the Sabbath."

The Pastor stood with a hunched over piety, like he was perpetually carrying something. And Clemency, though always respectful, couldn't help but be annoyed by the interruption.

"Well, Pastor," Burt said, rolling his eyes a little at Clemency, "I'm toiling for myself the other six days, so I figure the Lord won't mind me toiling for Him today."

Clemency's smile broadened, and it caught the eye of the Pastor.

"How 'bout this guy, he carrying his weight?"

Clemency hung his head.

"His weight and then some," Burt answered, not taking his eyes from his work.

"Well, I have to say I've been pleased to see him at service these past couple of months since…" The Pastor's voice wavered with a misstep that Clemency hadn't yet heard in the short time he'd known him.

Burt stopped working and looked to his nephew.

"What…what I mean to say is…" the Pastor stammered. Then he renewed his practiced tone, "The Bible says that a seed needs the proper soil to flourish, that it won't grow in barren sand."

Burt sighed.

"Clem, these pieces ain't meeting together quite right. You think you can put a little sharper angle on this one?" Burt said. He had already hoisted the piece into the air that separated him and his nephew.

Clemency wasn't about to refuse. He grabbed it and trotted over to the chop saw.

He laid the trim onto the saw, thought about where exactly his uncle was trying to put it, the image clear and sharp, and he shifted the setting to an estimated distance past forty-five degrees. He pulled the saw's trigger and brought it down against the grainy birch. With the blade singing, he heard a raised voice and glanced over to his uncle and the Pastor. Burt wasn't a terribly large man, but he was ample, with broad shoulders; and Clemency saw him leaning over the Pastor, his arm pointed in Clemency's direction, making sharp jabs with his sweating, muscular hand and finger. Clemency returned his eyes to his work, released the trigger, raised the piece of trim, and with a satisfied puff of air, blew the excess dust from his product. By the time he trotted back, the Pastor was walking toward his house.

He handed the trim over, and his uncle laid it in place.

"Goddamn, Clem!" Burt announced, no visible concern for the man of God sulking away. "Fits like it was born to it."

A few days later, Clemency got news that West Newton High School, where his mother and father had taught, in the next county—his father Literature, his mother Spanish—was set to hold a memorial service the coming Friday afternoon, to coincide with the fifteenth anniversary of when they had begun teaching there. Clemency attended Mossberg High School, his mother and father deciding against the undue pressure their son might encounter by having his parents at the same institution as himself.

Clemency's principal and teachers insisted that he attend, and that Friday morning Burt had caught a ride with his foreman and lent Clemency his truck. Cheryl was at work at the bank.

"I don't want them to know I'm here," Clemency told the Newton principal when he arrived. He was a tall, thin man with bushy eyebrows and pink cheeks, in a dark brown suit that hung from his bony shoulders. He told Clemency that that wouldn't be a problem, that he could just blend in among the students in the top bleachers.

"We sure are going to miss them," the principal added, his eyes already damp.

It was ten minutes into the presentation, exactly six photos of his mother smiling arm in arm with her colleagues in the lounge, and five photos of his father leaned back in his chair with his glasses pushed up onto his forehead, student after student beaming from across his desk, that Clemency headed back down the bleacher stairs. He nodded to the principal on his way out of the gymnasium and the sweet faced man just knowingly nodded back. A heavy set woman next to him had her face in her hands.

The tears there hadn't been in the past months came finally, and all at once. He got outside and collapsed against the coarse brick wall, his knees pulled to his chin.

Clemency walked then trotted toward the sun flooding through the glass of the distant line of doors. This school smelled different than Mossberg. There was a sour scent of overripe fruit, and polish. Clemency had never felt as far from his parents as right then. The tears there hadn't been in the past months came finally, and all at once. He got outside and collapsed against the coarse brick wall, his knees pulled to his chin.

A short, round man in jeans and a white dress shirt, struggling to put on a corduroy blazer and cursing under his breath, hurried from the parking lot.

"You're late," Clemency judged.

He would forever wonder why he'd said it.

"Are you all right?" the man said, slowing his awkward gait.

Clemency pulled his forearm across his nose and met the man's concerned eyes.

"Yeah, I'm fine."

"Clemency?"

Clemency grinned despite himself.

"Yes, sir."

"Well, you're the one I'm here to see," the man replied. He had now completely stopped and turned to face Clemency. "My name's Alan. Alan Gold. I'm…was a friend of your father's. God, you look just like him." He motioned with his fingers, "It's the eyes."

Clemency struggled up the wall.

"You don't have to get up"

"No, I need to," Clemency said, and pushed both palms past his temples.

Alan Gold told Clemency that he was a lawyer from Chicago with some business to discuss and invited him for a cup of coffee at the diner down the road that he had passed on his way in. Clemency glanced back through the doors, and accepted.

He watched the dusty haired Alan Gold sip his coffee and shuffle some papers on the table between them. Alan told him that he had gone to Purdue with his father; they had been roommates as freshmen and sophomores. They stayed in touch for a while after college but hadn't talked for a long time when Clemency's father had called him four years ago, out of the blue. He told Alan that he wanted him to handle the disbursement of their life insurance policy and meager savings account, if necessary, lest, through a small town manipulation of the law, either found its way into the care of his sister-in-law, Cheryl. He never trusted that woman.

"Now, those are his words, I remind you. I don't know your aunt," Alan insisted.

"How'd you know I'd be there today?" Clemency hadn't touched his coffee.

The lawyer donned a sheepish grin.

"Well, I called your parents' principal to inquire about any sort of service or memorial, and if you were attending, and let's just say a lawyer knows how to get the information he seeks."

"You threaten him?"

"No, no...I may have leaned on him a little."

Clemency tore the top from a sugar packet and poured it into his coffee, and he was pretty sure he didn't like Alan Gold, despite the fact that his father must have found something in the man to admire.

That's when the lawyer, with that same grin, slid the cashier's check for just under $56,000 between the cups to Clemency's side of the table.

"They didn't have much, but that's it. The paperwork's been taken care of. It's all there, minus my fee, of course."

Clemency thought about that fee: if it was what the lawyer had promised his dead father, and whom he might have leaned on to increase it.

"Well, Mr. Gold, I should really be going."

"Please. Alan, please." He froze. "Call me, Alan."

The red haired waitress breezed by and dropped the check on the table's edge.

"I got this," Alan said. And as he pulled the wallet from around his waist and struggled to pull a couple of crumpled bills from it, Clemency saw that his hands were shaking.

"You guys were good friends, huh?"

"The best," the lawyer acknowledged with a tremor in his speech. "Crazy times." Then he rested his hands on the table in front of him, like he was giving up. "I knew from the beginning I'd fuck this up somehow. I'd come on too strong, make you feel like you were being greased. I have a son about your age, a little younger. Your father's request got me thinking who I'd ask, if I needed something like this. Trust is a beautiful pain sometimes. Both giving it and getting it."

Alan waved his hands like, *don't listen to me*, and Clemency realized then that the grin hadn't been sheepish at all, only nervous. So he finally returned the smile.

"Alan, I think I should get this," Clemency said, and pulled a crisp twenty from his own wallet, the one Burt had insisted upon giving him on the ride home the previous Sunday evening. "Thank you."

Cheryl was livid. Burt and Clemency could hear her inside, pacing around, clacking and clattering everything she picked up or put down, certain they were listening; and, like good men, they were. The two stood on the concrete patio behind his aunt and uncle's house.

"You sure this is what you want?" Burt asked in earnest. "I mean, California? You know it ain't all like the movies, right?" There was a warning in his voice, sure, but a pleasant anticipation as well, like he hoped his nephew would say yes.

"Like the Pastor said, Uncle Burt, a seed can't grow in barren soil."

It was then that Clemency, though aware that things were now shaped the way he had shaped them, realized fully what he had decided to do. Burt dug deep into his pocket, his tongue between his teeth like he was driving home a nail, and pulled out a single key on a single ring, wound through a leather tab.

"Here. This'll save you a couple hundred at least."

It was the key to his truck.

"Uncle Burt..."

"Now, don't you say a word. I can catch a ride with my foreman till I get another. He smokes those goddamn Marlboros at six a.m., but he's always got a joke, every morning. And as for your Aunt Cheryl, well, I've disappointed her before and I've a feeling I'll do it again." Burt reached out and grabbed his nephew's hand, placing the key in his palm, and forcing his fingers to close around it.

"Just like his father!" they heard from inside. They shared a guilty laugh.

"You know, Uncle Burt, there isn't too many people who—"

"Now, hold on, I got something else."

Burt disappeared through his garage door. Clemency could hear him rattling around in the shelves above his workbench. Then he reappeared, in the dim, blue glow of the bug light. He had something that looked like a vinyl textbook in his hands. It was a bible.

"Burt, I don't know if I—"

"Now, hold on there." Clemency saw then that his uncle was crying. The tears must have started while he was in the garage, searching for the parting gift. "Ain't a lot of people had the life you've had in the last couple of months. And against my best, natural instincts, you've been privy to too much of what's right and what's wrong. But I want you to remember something," Burt pulled a sharp, tenuous breath through an oddly masculine whimper, "there ain't no right and wrong, Clemency Parker, not in this world, there's just what is, and what ain't. And this here book only helps when you read it for yourself."

..."there ain't no right and wrong, Clemency Parker, not in this world, there's just what is, and what ain't."

Clemency held the book in his hand, seeming to weigh it.

"Look," Burt started again, "without it, we're just animals."

But aren't we anyway? Clemency wanted to ask, but chose not to.

Jerry took the mountain curve way too fast, and Clemency's muscles tightened. He had to admit to himself that the enormous Ford was so much steel and rubber that it could probably roll down the steep incline to his right with ease, or because of its size come out of an accident with its passengers intact. So he concentrated on the Sierra Nevada, tall and dark and cut by nature into deep, flat valleys and exposed granite. The whole damn thing bathed in setting sun. He let out an impressed sigh for how unlike Indiana it was.

"Gorgeous, ain't it?" Jerry said.

"Yeah," Clemency answered. "It's crazy, but all my time in that valley, and I've never been up here at dusk."

The road bent sharply and the cab filled with an orange light breaking between a cloud and the peak below it.

"Well, if you'd taken me up on that deal, you could've moved up here," Jerry said with his trademarked condescending smirk; he downshifted.

"Yes, Wilkins, we all know you're rich," Clemency said, his eyes back out the window.

"Don't do that. Don't shrug me off like that. This is a world for those that take it, Parker. With *man* smack dab in the middle of it. You go around meek and mild and you'll never get anything you want. No matter how many weekends they make you work."

"Yeah."

"No, really. Hell, I spend more time hunting and fishing these days than I ever did working. Cause I took what I wanted. I'm the center of my universe. Nobody tells me when I work and when I don't."

"Actually," Clemency said, "I volunteer most weekends. Not for free. But I'm not asked to be there."

"You're there willingly?!" Jerry turned town the AM station, Don Williams crooning in Tulsa-time. "That blows my mind."

"Really?" Clemency said.

"I mean, Jesus, a man would have to love his job quite a bit to be that committed, or that stupid." The smirk was back.

Clemency cracked his window to let a rush of cool fresh air into the cab.

"Not his job," Clemency admitted, "just his work," and left it at that.

Later, Jerry Wilkins pointed in a general direction and told Clemency, good luck.

Clemency trudged though the ankle high snow. He'd learned rather quickly after the "you should have taken me up conversation," that he wasn't Jerry's first choice. Wouldn't really have been a choice at all had Jerry's friends not simply bailed out of the hunting trip. Wilkins was just over-confident he'd take some massive kill and wanted someone around to help him get it back to the truck.

Clemency pulled up the jeans under his Carhartts. He looked up and saw Orion, brandishing his quarry. A week before his parents went to dinner up north, his father had declared to teach him a constellation a week, said it was something he'd neglected for too long; in the end, they'd only gotten time for the first lesson. Would he kill something today, and gut it? Jerry had briefed him on the gruesome details, in the unlikely event. Bring the blade anus to throat, with as much care and as little pressure as he could muster. Then quarter the carcass.

He passed the fossils of a used-to-be deerblind. There were two rusty nails protruding from a weathered tread that was being swallowed by the tree. Clemency walked over and touched each, back and forth, rubbed them with his gloved hand until they crumbled away under his attentions.

On the cold wind was the smell of fruit, carried up on a wisp from the valley, and then gone.

Clemency's legs were tired and, crouching, he leaned against the roots of a lone elm. Within minutes, from a nearby stand of pines, across a small clearing, a buck improbably emerged. It stood there. The air was still light enough to see the beast's nostrils billowing steam.

There was a weight in Clemency's stomach like he'd swallowed a bomb.

He raised the borrowed rifle to aim from his position against the tree. Through the scope, he could see the muscle of the deer he would harvest if he pulled the trigger, the shoulders and back, the prideful breast, all sitting steaming on his table, attended by a hungry neighbor, and his own hungry wife: Wilkins is hunched in his chair, nursing a sore back from his part in dragging this meal back to the truck. Carol, with a concealed elbow, pushes the mauve bible off the table. Clemency zeroed the crosshairs just behind the buck's shoulder, like Wilkins had said. Drawing a secret breath, the strangest thought occurred to him: he thinks of Jesus the man, the carpenter. Wonders if he was able to concentrate on what was in front of him. Thinks of him leaning over his materials and enjoying the pain of a splinter. Watches him create and bevel to near perfection the very device that would be his death. Then Clemency sees his own scene from above. He sees himself and the buck and the trees and snow that envelop them. He sees the flash from the barrel. He watches the animal fall.

Kristofer Whited was born in Wheatfield, Indiana. He received his Bachelor's degree at Purdue University and his MFA at California State University Fresno. He has worked on the editorial staffs of Sycamore Review *and* The Normal School *and has taught fiction, creative writing, and composition. His work has appeared in* Monkey Puzzle, Octave, *and* Connotation Press. *He now lives in Denver, Colorado and teaches composition and technical writing at Community College of Aurora.*

Cornelius Eady

Overturned

What did you hear today
That got you talking raw?
You got that low cloud look,
Got that heart nicked stare.

Like the flora got voted
From under your feet.
Like someone told you a story,

Maybe it's the wrong story,
Palm trees where there should
Be pine. And now you doubt

Everything. Don't you hate
Doubting everything? There's
An unease the body radiates

When it can't put a finger
On a lie. You got that pickle
Wince, my friend,

You look like
You lost the directions
To where you from.

Deep Song

These mother-fuckers,
These mother-fuckers
Won't let me sing.
Billie Holiday
Will not be allowed
To raise her voice
At Lester Young's funeral.
She won't be allowed.
She is a scarlet woman.
The mourners, the mourners
Are scandalized.
He was sweet,
And now he's gone.
He was hers,
And his wife won't have it.
These mother-fuckers.
These mother-fuckers.
That's love.
That the understanding
Of how long he's been gone,
How long he'll be gone.
It's deep, down in her cells.
It's awful, just terrible.
Right in a church
She's showing it.
Right in a church.
What you going do about it,
Harlem?
That voice

That broken-bottle neck
Voice
She want his sax
Around her voice cords
She wants his pork-pie
Pulled rough against
Her skin, her body
Is a horn. Let me sing
About love, she thunders
Let me sing about love
You mother fuckers.

Cornelius Eady was born in 1954 in Rochester, New York. He is the author of several books of poetry, including the critically acclaimed Hardheaded Weather *(Penguin, 2008), which was nominated for an NAACP Image Award. His other titles are* Â Kartunes, *(Warthog Press, 1980);* Victims of the Latest Dance Craze, *(Ommation Press, 1986), winner of the 1985 Lamont Prize from the Academy of American Poets;* The Gathering of My Name, *(Carnegie Mellon University Press, 1991), nominated for the 1992 Pulitzer Prize in Poetry;* You Don't Miss Your Water, *(Henry Holt and Co., 1995);* The Autobiography of a Jukebox *(Carnegie-Mellon University Press, 1997); and* Brutal Imagination *(Putnam, 2001). His work appears in many journals; magazines; and the anthologies* Every Shut Eye Ain't Asleep, In Search of Color Everywhere, *and* The Vintage Anthology of African American Poetry, *(1750-2000) ed. Michael S. Harper. With poet Toi Derricote, Eady is cofounder of Cave Canem, a national organization for African American poetry and poets.*

Klaus Martens

from Alter Knochen Spricht
(Old Crock Speaks)

Old Geezers

There are a couple of old geezers
a bit older than, younger than or maybe of my generation.
They were banned from practicing their professions
or weren't "re-purposed," as they used to say,
and they wanted to become teachers
or journalists
if they couldn't do anything else,
or because they were good teachers and journalists,
or wanted to become them,
and knew a thing or two.
Children and readers trotted around enthusiastically behind these geezers
who didn't think much of the rules
but thought a lot of themselves;
who ran the tip of their tongues across their lips,
pondered, grinned, then wrote or spoke.
You'd recognize them by the intellectual-looking, standard-issue glasses
they like to wear on the tips of their noses,
or by their cheerful irony, sunken cheeks
or wobbly bellies.
They go around like Tintin
in baggy pants with rivets,
of the not pre-washed sort, from *C&A*
(on sale), shirts from *Penny*,
well worn-in tweed jackets and well-worn

but freshly nuanced sayings:
Oh yeah, you really mean that, man?
Some craft poems like Erich Fried's
and hum along to the guitar in a post-revolutionary fog.
Despite all that.
Sentimental? *Claro*, a little,
but weren't we right? Look, folks,
the opposition is always right,
halfways,
but these guys in particular—
even if nobody really rightly remembers.

Vespers

The warm, wet wings of the evening sink
semi-transparent, silver and grey, down along the towers
of St. James in Toronto and onto the trees
of the almost abandoned park, not far from this bench.

Back from the movies, my dinner in a plastic bag
next to me on the seat. A bolt of lightening penetrates
the hovering haze and lands a little bit in front of me.
All this twirling, this striding, her stare—

She is my seagull, still unfamiliar, but mine.
She found me, one among all the others
who are not eating. I am her friend and must
share everything now. Here, a crumb, and another one.

Further bolts alight. My seagull
cranes her neck horizontally, opens her beak
and speaks loudly. We want to be left alone, we
friends, for the infinity of our vespers.

from Abwehrzauber (Enchanting Resistance)

Wiggle Room

There are moments, waking or sleeping,
in which the fit between the seed and the shell loosens,

as with a hazelnut, when desiccation
shrinks the kernel, allows it to shift.

When the aged skin is just a loose mantle
for flesh and bone and seems foreign,
mimics clothing,

like on a Zen-Ascetic, hunger artist,
or a time-withered, dying stranger.

When something opens up
between you and your frame
as between layers of an onion,
like rooms

in mortality, in which you are cold, alone,
not armed with your accoutrements.

No ecstasy, you are not out of your mind—
no, you are approaching inner fission,
becoming alien,

free from your well-tested self,
that old soul, that now reveals itself.

Iceland on my Mind

Iceland has everything that it needs
and no more—
these volcanoes, geysers; it is
a modest land.

When you don't expect it,
you see, emerging from the bottom of the heart,
unfathomably, the smile of an icy ocean,
freezing, yet never frozen.

Under the clear-glass moon white frost
lies on the shaggy coat
of the Icelandic horses
with their quilted riders,
lonesome, nightly wayfarers.

Iceland has everything that it needs.
It is not the south—
Its names clarify familial relationships.
Daughter of Thule, of Greenland.

I wish I had been in Iceland
and had simply stayed there,
legendarily lonesome and proud
on the upper edge of consciousness.

Home is

Where nobody expects you
where nobody recognizes you.

Where others inhabit your street
where others live in your house.

Where you haven't been in a long time,
where your childhood just played itself out.

Where home no longer exists,
where you no longer belong.

Home is thinking about home.
Home is where your head is.

Klaus Martens is the author of nine books of poetry: Heimliche Zeiten *(1984),* Angehaltenes Schweigen *(1985),* Im Wendekreis des Fragezeichens *(1987),* Die Fähre und 14 andere Gedichte *(2006),* Gedichte 1984-2010 *(online publication by fixPoetry.com),* Das wunderbare Draußen *(2010),* Alter Knochen spricht *(2011),* Abwehrzauber *(2012) and* Schwedenbuch *(2011). His new book,* Siebenachtel Leben: Aus dem Arbeitsbuch *will be published in 2014 as part of an exhibition of Martens' work in celebration of his 70th birthday.*

Muriel Cormican, translator, is a professor of German and film at the University of West Georgia. She is the author of the monograph Negotiating Identity: Women in the Works of Lou Andreas-Salomé *and of several critical articles on contemporary German film and literature. She spends at least ten weeks every year in Oldenburg, Germany, mentoring and teaching students on UWG's German Study Abroad Program.*

Kurtis Lamkin

Safiya

All hail Garvey Park
thousand people in the sun
you give them your poem
and they shine, sunshine
Safiya

The world is shaped like a hug to them
they keep giving it their all
who will tell their struggles
if you go - don't go
Safiya, Safiya

On stage
barefoot
dreadlock
red dress
they look at you to see how far you'll go
you look at them to see how far they've come:
across the water
thru the fire
over mountaintops
into stars

You are their daughter
who will tell their struggles
if you go? Don't go.
Safiya

Drought

The drought
has ended

in this moist
night

heaven has
landed

so why
am I

holding
only myself

and rocking?

Kurtis Lamkin is a poet from Philadelphia who plays the kora and the jinjin, harp-like string instruments. He has performed nationally and internationally on stage, radio, film and television. Many of his poems have been published widely in magazines, journals and anthologies.

His animated poem, "The Foxes Manifesto," about the Soweto Rebellion in South Africa, aired for two years on PBS. He has produced several cds, the latest of which is called Kora Poems. *He currently lives in Charleston, South Carolina.*

Eric Smith

Hey

Well-wishers, if you still stand with your coin
waiting to huck your coveting's mute glimmer
into the unwrinkled water—well, here we are.

Go nuts. We always begin with a burden
of quiet, admiring silence's needlework
stitched into this space between us.

For this I have loved your ingenious hands.
To those slumped into boredom's plushness,
save your lighter for someone else's encore.

I am still me. Peel back this Halloween mask.
Take my hand for as long as it takes
to get through this, my jacket to persuade

the skittish chill it wasn't worth the effort.
Let my voice unravel its thinning yarn
to the exit of this hour, and all the hours
I learned to want before I learned that want
is the belly's lie. As little birds of applause
leave your palms to flit among the lights,

forgetful as water and time's slow shuffle,
begin again this last, futile correspondence.
Hey. Good morning. It's been real. Hey.

Hey

begins with dignity, borne on a silver tray,
among a hubbub of calling cards that say
nothing despite Byzantine loops of calligraphy.
As it throws open the double doors of dentistry,
the squeak-free gears of its machinery
unburden your mouth's tumblers. Now free,
flattering dollops of light fall into the martini
glass of the *y*. Beautifully curved and glittery,
downhome diphthong in strapless Versace—
always a smash, even among the cognoscenti.
But we had long forgotten its monosyllabic lie,
how eagerly it dismisses us, its *trompe-l'oeil.*
It sidles up to the unwary, forever blasé,
to begin yet again its facile parley.

Hey.

Hey

Whichever failures condescend tonight
from a firmament strung with chandeliers,
or startle into wakefulness under houselights
wearing the dusty sleeves of untouched years,
the error's forever mine. Put away polite

applause, because none of this outlasts us.
When the bulbs burn down at last, we are
the filament, and all the tear-stained faces
blinking toward an exit. Self-aware, we wear
out wariness as gas lamps lick the last blue hiss.

So, hey. Come here. Put your ear to my mouth.
If you hold your breath, you'll hear the sea.
In another life, you would have been a house
of rain, and I the wind unwinding in your eaves.
Listen to my ocean as it gives, and gives out.

Eric Smith's poems appear or are forthcoming in Indiana Review, The Journal, *and* Southwest Review. *He teaches at Marshall University and edits* cellpoems.

Seth Michelson

Vencerémos: A Manifesto

—for Víctor Jara

They snapped your fingers, one
by one, pain
exploding from each
busted knuckle, till
only the agony
of your hand
was real and present.
All that remained
was the echo
of bone
snapped
and crooked fingers
in pain like snakes
on fire, your hand
a butterfly
stitched alive
into a sweaty collector's
leather-bound book,
one more specimen
captured, pinned down
to die here, where
thousands are being beaten
all around you, here
in Estadio Chile,
that civic cathedral
where the Comandante
rasps, *You'll never again*
sing or strum, Víctor,

as if a mess of insults
and mangled fingers
and crazy bullets
could kill a song.

Seth Michelson currently lives in Los Angeles, California. Just as he has enjoyed living in many places (Baltimore, Buenos Aires, Helsinki, Montevideo, New York City, Sydney, and elsewhere), he also has enjoyed many jobs (bouncer, janitor, journalist, limo driver, pizza maker, professor, and more). His poetry has appeared in journals across the country, and he is the author of the book Eyes like Broken Windows *and chapbooks* Maestro of Brutal Splendor, Kaddish for My Unborn Son, *and* House in a Hurricane. *He also is the translator of the book of poetry* El ghetto, *by Argentine poet Tamara Kamenszain.*

Afaa Michael Weaver

Da Mo Meets Ronald McDonald

In the far off lights that speak to saints,
he heard of the tall man in red yellow rings,
a clown who is not a clown, a man who
is not a man, a beacon calling to saints,
waking the Buddha so that Da Mo took
the roads down from the cave to the streets
full of students and old men, made his way
in his old clothes and sandals, ignoring fingers
held to noses against the smell of gods
who sit in silence without showers or shaving
for centuries, the years gone by, forests
dying and being born, ignoring the way children
point at dark foreigners and saints like slivers
of light that bounce themselves off from heaven.

Quarter pounders and Big Macs, fries,
the whole carnival of what lines the tubes
inside the heart were there when they met,
Ronald for the moment come to life, sitting
up out of the porcelain way of being a statue,
seeing Taipei's afterlife when night is let down
and men go off to see the women without voice,
children asleep or reading gongfu novels
with flashlights, forgetting the characters
of language, Ronald this watchman, paragon
of stillness, Da Mo the light from India
walking into the eye of China's circle way
of winding around itself, the magpie settling
on the backs of fans, women so beautiful
they shame meadows and green mountains.

America, a Challenge to Love

We undo tiny things, sighs from a baby ant under
a hair, in the clump of grass, what the knoll knows,
as if the knoll belongs, its thin places swollen like
gluttons bracing for false gums, what aches when teeth
awaken to the fact of being abandoned, the raw truth
of only tooth to bone like waking up in a nightmare
that replaces grocery shopping, getting a haircut,
losing your sex organ in intercourse, the open air
facts we'd rather not know, the obvious not-being
lying beneath the skin in autopsies on YouTube,
making fun of Dr Frankenstein to say *it's alive*,
knowing to say so is to lie about what lives if it really
is alive because nothing like that can live, insincere
sense of smiles hiding the next move on the board
where we gather, which has to be small or has
to be nothing, a place where emptiness draws out
desire hidden in a fantasy called friendship, *rock me
until midnight is gone*, while a cup as light as air
holds the unloved, the tiny things swirling inside us.

Cold Mountain and the Maiden

In the way mud oozes through the toes
of children running in the rain, he slides
into Starbucks, the most unkind mark
of history, Mandarin the only gesture
he knows is China, and she comes soon
after, in the glow, leaning against him,
not knowing immortal skin, immortal air.
Time tells him to tell her, and he puts
a spell into things, names this the moment
to tell all, to list the lines in the walls
of the cave, to give out the secret of life,
how it winds itself into us, spins itself
out of us, the prime number key to heaven
and nothingness. In his eyes, she sees
madness, the too still deepness, rude hair,
unkempt way of a Chinese she has never
known, falling into the spell, coffee made
all around her, latte, mocha, caramel,
every caffeine blessing, the patrons
blind to the sage in the homeless man.
He takes her to a table, pulls her down
to the chair with one finger, his breath
cloaking itself in some spring fantasy
hiding the mouth with no teeth, the hands
gnarled from walking sticks with handles
crude the way laughter in the mountains
ignores the rules of manners, the city
now like cities he knows, his spell a law
that brings back the simple ring of things,

night bells in the neighborhood, the toll
of old bones tapping stones in walkways
where the new cries out for what is gone.

Afaa Michael Weaver (born Michael S. Weaver), a native of Baltimore, has been a Pew fellow, a Fulbright scholar in Taiwan, and an NEA fellow in poetry. His first book of poetry Water Song, *was published in 1985 by U Press of Virginia. He has had plays produced professionally and worked as an editor and freelance journalist. His short fiction is included in the anthology* Children of the Night. *His eleventh collection of poems is* Kama i'reeh (Like the Wind) *(2010) a translation of his work into Arabic by Wissal Al-Allaq. Weaver works as an editor and a translator, principally in Chinese. At Simmons College he holds an endowed chair as Alumnae Professor of English. In 2004 and 2008, he convened two international conferences of Chinese poets at Simmons, the first such conferences ever held outside China. Weaver is recognized in the Chinese poetry community as one of America's major supporters of contemporary Chinese poetry. In 2005 the Chinese Writers Association in Beijing gave him a gold friendship medal.*

He maintains a translation website called Poets Cafe at: www.transpoet.com In March 2013 his twelfth collection of poetry, The Government of Nature, *was published by U of Pittsburgh Press. His personal website is: www.afaamweaver.com. Weaver lives in Somerville, Massachusetts.*

Malachi Black

Ode to Potions

Somewhere even now / a cedar press
is edging down / to separate new sugar

from the able-bellied grape / to ease
each swelling blister of the dusk

it yields / this ink / purpling my raw throat
past its pink / manifesting red

webs in my eyes // I've followed each
infinitely curled herb's countless recipes

for sleep / tinctured chamomile / dead passionflower /
skullcap / kava root / ground lavender /

valerian / warm lemon balm // Exhausting
powders and elixirs / I've tried all

pills and all prescription drugs / there is nothing
to be done // Tonight I raise my wine jug / to the sun

[If it is]

If it is
emptiness

that lifts
a buoy

above
the sotted

waterline
then let me be

as empty
as the sky

Malachi Black is the author of Storm Toward Morning, *forthcoming from Copper Canyon Press, and two limited edition chapbooks:* Quarantine *(Argos Books, 2012) and* Echolocation *(Float Press, 2010). The current Creative Writing Fellow in Poetry at Emory University, Black has also received fellowships and awards from the Bread Loaf Writers' Conference, the Corporation of Yaddo, the Fine Arts Work Center in Provincetown, The MacDowell Colony, the Poetry Foundation, the Sewanee Writers' Conference, the University of Texas at Austin's Michener Center for Writers, and the University of Utah.*

Dana Inez

Letters from an Expatriate

Dear Sty, *Concerning Sterility*;

Germany is gorgeous, sunshine every day and the beaches are to die for. I think I'm forming delusions LOL. In an alternate universe we are all pharmacists. There's a pill that rids you of emotional debts. In this world they will never find you if you change your phone number. I've gone to Germany because of the bankruptcy laws among other things. Now because we are pharmacists we are moving our hands across sterile tables at a rate comparable to an ultimate efficiency.

Dear Sty, *Concerning Hydration*;

The dreams are occurring in groups of four and I'm dead or else all my friends are. A spontaneous post-bomb post-scare and Meredith Snow is flying down the avenue flanked by eight of my worst enemies in weight order gargling salt water LOL. Welcome to Germany Meredith Snow would you like some water how about some heart how about some value how about some sea salt fresh from the freshly painted cabinet.

Dear Sty, *Concerning Oklahoma*;

We were flying over Oklahoma thinking of the United Nations. We were thinking about the United Nations while tearing up inside. If you agree to the notion, you will get one five-cent thirty-second glimpse of your high school boyfriend shooting lines and then a bonus forty-five seconds of him seducing his underage cousin. This is all for only five cents but you have to act now.

Dear Sty, *Concerning Dirty Stories;*

Shell-shocked Meredith Snow has gained on me so I'll have to pick up the pace. It's difficult to visualize disregard. It's nice to be indebted to people and not systems. She's stolen my lines and then my effaced morality. Shrug and curtail the source. I like these dirty stories I like these dirty stories I like them. It's funny how news travels fast until someone's dead or conversely how new travels fast until someone's alive.

Dear Sty, *Concerning Sucking;*

In a letter dated August 9, I write, "Dear Sty, Oklahoma is filled with idolaters, greasyboys, misers filled with pounds of wisdom." Excuse, for once, someone else besides me. We aren't isolationists. When half of its citizens are somewhere else it's hardly a country. If you are fighting for the freedom of someone else you are that someone else. Don't be jealous, this is all in real time. It's steadily in real time and more or less done. I'm familiar with the notion and agree it must suck to suck. Germany is gorgeous, sunshine every day and the beaches are to die for.

Dear Sty, *Concerning Magnificence;*

I was lounging when you saw me last and I've been embarrassed ever since. Here are the semantics: Suburban Warfare in a lot of ways. The only difference between me and him albeit a strange morality is three beers and anyone ever. Meredith Snow and I watched the hoarders today. At least they own their Consumer Choices. At least they're Loyal. As for Meredith Snow, she's at it again that little slut. Have to tell her to stay where she belongs. She's getting Chunky. No one is Appreciating it Everything is pointing to me Being Right. Consider this notification that this is something I live with constantly.

Dear Sty, *Concerning Falling*;

I'll question anything I can't get my hands on. Suburban Warfare is infiltrating our supermarkets our showers our sexualities. If my sexuality falls in a place where no one is does it make a sound? Is it there to begin with? This is Germany, Sty. That you've ever been here I doubt it.

Dear Sty, *Concerning Exhaustion*;

Having low biorhythms is just a fancy word for wanting to take a nap. Meredith Snow's looking slutty again LOL. I think she's getting sick of me or possibly scared of me. If her ambitions are evident, if she's a great and intelligent woman, I'm sorry. If not, I'm still sorry. This is a picture of Meredith Snow in the prime of her life. In other news, Germans are sunny and beautiful and the beaches are to die for.

Dear Sty, *Concerning Abortion*;

The only Germany I can't stand is Abortion Germany. JKing,

not a real place. Since young, have been obsessed with words language linguistics topology. Since young, have been JKing. Since young Meredith Snow has been hateful. If anything bad happens she can blame it on that. This is comfort.

Dear Sty, *Concerning Joy*;

In a letter dated March 17, I write, "Moderation weakens you." I still agree with myself. Today at the supermarket I told a man to control his woman. I think people should be forced to stay inside their homes and watch the massacre from abroad. In response, the man asks if I'm in good health because I look skinnier than last year. I don't know if this is true or a ploy to get me thinking. Sty, you'd never do that to me you heap of joy you.

Dear Sty, *Concerning Good*;

In a letter dated January 2, I write, "I'm saving up for Oklahoma to buy a house and die." This was three years ago today. I am now in Germany taking advantage of the gorgeous beaches. This is a reduction technique: take one and have the other. We are only given what we can handle and apparently I can't handle anything. One day I will want to write to you about love and one day I will want to be happy all the time. I'm superficially concerned with my body and my future. Have some friends who are so good it scares you, Sty. So good it scares the years right from you.

Dear Sty, *Concerning Scared*;

To answer the question dated June 6, yes of course they'd

hear my sexuality fall. When someone's mean to you just imagine his best friend from college just died. That's what I do. I've received word, Sty. Congratulations on the reconciling of your many emotions that surface in different situations. I am aware of the face value of your new strange morality. In other news, Germany is in it to win it, Germany isn't ready for the long haul, Germany isn't demanding your time. It is sunny and gorgeous and the beaches, the beaches.

Dear Sty, *Concerning War*;

Last night I dreamt I finally had access to Meredith Snow's email so I could monitor her ways. I'm competing with her. As for the letter you sent dated September 9, I'm not sure about the use of the word loyalty. Though a little loyalty would be nice. I find in the German population an obsession with/affinity for making noise and hearing themselves make noise. It's deplorable really, a real hoot a real entertainment. Sty, you and I both know that you know nothing about baseball. You're skinny, you never once played an organized team sport, and you rarely if ever use your arms. Let's take the time to remember when you landed in Oklahoma after the war and people asked you what was your favorite part and you said watching the hot girls walk around the University of Baghdad. You know nothing about baseball. In regards to my ongoing pursuit for country, I'm breaking out in lacerations. I'm nobody's child.

Dear Sty, *Concerning Total Life*;

You are god as my witness. Welcome to Germany. Here is

where the beaches are to die for. If you look to your left, you'll find my amputations. If you look to your right, you'll find Total Life. I enjoy the energy of the fight. I rarely if ever use my intellect for good. Do you believe in monolithic characters? Do you believe in yourself? I won't sit here and beg you to come. But the beaches Sty, the beaches.

Dear Sty, *Concerning Childhood*;

Don't give the answer to the question Sty because it's confusing. Childhood is a soft whispering. If it can't be quantified it can rarely if ever be Germany. Meredith Snow is contrived. Hello Meredith Snow, hello sweet girl. The boys found her gruesome, dealt with it anyway. I mind Sty, I mind about this, and I entirely fill up attention.

Dear Sty, *Concerning Medication*;

If you join me in Germany now, we will call it:

1. Our Highly Medicated Trip Through Europe
2. Our Highly Tractable Trip Through Europe
3. Our Highly Conversational Trip Through Europe
4. Our Highly Lacerable Trip Through Europe
5. Our Fucking Trip Through Europe
6. Our Highly Imaginable Trip Through Europe
7. Our Highly Gorgeous Trip Through Europe

Remember when you're in Oklahoma, you're even screwing up in the supermarket. How about some torch fuel how about some dental floss how about some feeling.

Dear Sty, *Concerning Sake*;

>What's known is known. What's known is up for grabs. Real world problems have found their way into my heart, my mind, my near sexual organs. On February 21 I wrote, "Drink up for complex sexualities and 1.5 kids." Meredith Snow's taken on a new form, a place for the thrift of mind with no respect for the masthead. In Oklahoma, I'd laugh before crying but in Germany we think twice before doing either. There is a sake in trying doing suggesting and the beaches, the beaches.

Dear Sty, *Concerning Economy*;

>It's technically raining on all parades if you want to think of it personally. It's 2013 and we are still seven degrees removed from our insides. To answer your question dated July 17, yes of course you can. On doing it right, it's okay. I love the energy of the fight minus any typefaces or small computer-generated images. I am interested in feeding tubes LOL. What they do for the economy the economists the economically downtrodden.

Dear Sty, *Concerning Family*;

>Forget about dirty stories. This is the upscale classic big mistake of our lives. Dear friends of the family. Dear friends of our father's family. Dear friends of our mother's family. Dear friends of our sister's family. Dear friends let us out let us feel let us breathe in the fresh air of Germany. Hello Sty welcome welcome. That you've ever been here I doubt it.

Dear Sty, *Concerning Retrospect*;

> Believability is key. Largeness is key. This is all in real time and happening. If you take Meredith Snow's language away, she'll come begging for it back. I'm never concerned with Holy Books. I believe in God because I don't believe in myself. I stand my own mind day after day after day after. Who wins who does not operate on fear? I understand we usually exclude nothing. These are my suggestions. I look back with Pure Happiness in Retrospect. Germans are gorgeous Sty, and the beaches are to die for.

Dear Sty, *Concerning Hands*;

> This is my last confession. When asked, "If a lot of things burn in a fire what burns in a fire," it seems that Americans have trouble answering "a lot of things." In Oklahoma it seems like there's been a falling out. Consolation 1 is that they can't hear what you're thinking. Consolation 2 is it's better than last year. I'm struggling here. You're the worst news I've heard all day. I'm fiddling all around now. I'm doing a lot of shit with my hands. Are you American Sty, are you pretty pretty.

Dear Sty, *Concerning Nature*;

> Straight faced irony is. Straight laced physicality is. Enough about Oklahoma. If you can't stand your own mind come here. The air is useless. The ground has been dyed a color least often associated with nature. On the walls hang strange regalia purporting change. Strange regalia purporting The New Life. Strange regalia purporting cancer, the pros and

cons of it being on the inside of you.

Dear Sty, *Concerning Poverty*;

Regarding parenthetically dismantling Oklahoma, okay. This is shorthand for the range of my feelings. It's about time to put the air conditioner in. It's about time to shower in the dark. Are you interested in timing, Sty. The inevitable stuck while practicing it. We've forgotten whole pharmacies in our expensive cabinets. We've forgotten whole personalities in our expensive sick. Do you like sunsets, Sty. How about feelings. This job will give you a lifestyle similar to mine. I'm a fragile child. I wouldn't do these things unless provoked too much in too little time. By the age of seven, children in Germany have already figured out they have to lie to be funny. These dirty stories concern only that.

Dana Inez received her MFA from Sarah Lawrence College and currently lives in New York. Her poems have recently appeared in Bone Bouquet Journal, Two Serious Ladies, *and* Crack the Spine. *Her fiction is forthcoming in* Unsaid.

G. Taylor Davis & Sebastián Páramo

Minty Fresh

I'm a huge fuck—
leave my heart out on the pine…
It hurts to touch this pillow.
Your hotel has run out of mints.
You've gone. I seek combs of honey
in another saccharine date.

The hairs on my temples date
me, but I do not give a fuck
if you offer up your honey
anymore. Whores are numerous as pine
trees. You know, I only drink your mint
tea out of sympathy. You take my pillows:

You wash all my pillows
out of habit. As if we still date.
Remember when our love was mint
and fresh. We could never fuck
enough. The showers after smelled like pine.
But you threw me out, honey.

I cannot forget that honey
is at times too sweet And pillows
are softer to touch than pine.
My planner is free, you can date
a donkey for all I care. Fuck—
fucking, fuck your mints!

Fucking mints!
Fucking honeys!
Fucking fucks!
Fucking pillows!
Fucking dates!
Fucking pines!

Forget it, I have no need to pine
for days and mistakes I never meant.
Another invitation in the mail: *Save the Date.*
I break a glass, spill honey
wine on the shirt next to the pillow—
fuck.

I still buy dates and pine nuts at the store.
I fuck, I clean my mouth with mints.
But you can stop washing my pillows now, honey.

G. Taylor Davis, Jr is a graduate of Sarah Lawrence College's MFA program in writing. He received his BA from the University of North Carolina at Wilmington. In the past, his work has appeared in The Boiler Journal, La Fovea, *and* The Atlantis. *He hails from the Milky Way, but currently lives in Thailand.*

Sebastián Páramo

Drunk

The bar is closed. You can't drive
& the buses don't run late enough.
You spent all your drinking money,
your wife just left you & you worked all day
for an asshole—who can't even wipe his own ass.

It's Sunday. The bartender doesn't give
a damn if you keep the tab open or hears
your gripe and bitch about that old
sweetheart of yours. The story's been washed
so many times it doesn't even look stained.

Folks say it's cheaper to drink at home.
Finish all the whiskey in the cabinets. But
what are you going to do for a nightcap then?
Didn't want to drink alone. Everyone is gone
& you've stumbled out into the streets like a fuck up.

You thought you could handle relationships,
the walk home, but why does the pavement
in this dark alley appear so comfortable?

Sebastián H Páramo hails from Texas and his poems have appeared in The Oklahoma Review, Lunch Ticket, Used Furniture Review, *and others. He's an editor for the online journal,* The Boiler. *He currently teaches writing in New York.*

Doug Babington

The More Clothes You Buy, the More I Will Always Think of You Naked

On the eve of the demonstration we made love.
I cupped your backside in my palms
And rehearsed explosions on the street.

Weeks passed as society went to hell.
February's storm tore oranges from the trees,
We all mourned the shopkeeper's suicide,

And then you went away.

Only motorbikes roar in protest now,
Only tourists read political news.
I wait for you in the village square,
Imagining the chic boutiques
And you,
Naked,
No matter the gowns he has you buy.

Doug Babington is an American writer based in Montreal, Quebec. He taught American literature and academic writing for 30 years at Queen's University in Kingston, Ontario. He also directed the university's writing program. Doug has co-authored three books on the craft of writing, as well as travel essays and academic articles in journals such as Queen's Quarterly *and* The Journal of Modern Greek Studies.

Shawn Delgado

Groucho Marx Joke

Have you heard the one where Groucho says, *I don't care*
to belong to any club that will have me as a member?

I think of it some nights, when I'm unwelcome even in my own bed.
I tell myself, not tonight, *go sleep on the couch*

where I lie in the dark, watch TV next to a half-drunk beer
while 2AM recycles the 10PM movie into the dead air.

My favorite number is one hundred. When paired with a %,
it becomes tangible infinity, great mountains in the distance

on a flat road, but a small tank of gas. I can see it,
can touch it with my eyes, but there's no way I'll make it there

to the place of easy sleep, where *try your hardest*
doesn't have to mean exhausted-death like the first marathon.

My body-bound hands get jealous of my eyes, blame me since
I fidget as they shine a light in my face, ask me about my idleness.

This morning, I asked a sidewalk stranger for the time. He frowned as
    he lost
a few steps to deliver an answer. *Just give him what he wants*

so he'll shut up. I roll in my sleep, bump the remote
and hear a voice: infomercial lullaby, tell me again about $99.95

in five-easy-payments. My debt can't be capped at a single sum;
it's a wound, the gap between *could have* and *did*

V-ing wider with time. I want exhaustion: to sleep spent, penniless
and limp. This sleep only feels broke, gets shorter each night.

Before the Bang

In the Beginning, our bodies were so whole
we were holy—unformed energy in a ball smaller than any sun,
yet all the suns were there with every son of the reptiles
and all the dancing daughters of water and light.
Small enough to be emptiness, our center held each worm and root.
Every quasar. Every skyscraper. Every rock.
All pets, past and present, rested by the lost keys,
even the ones still not lost. All was potential
as the universe churned in its womb.
The Angelfish were years from being
Angelfish, and metal elements hadn't been invented,
needing to sort-out their arrangements. My hands had to live
countless lives in darkness—in caves and fields, in castles and cities
—wringing their atoms for eons as they waited to become hands.
For my lifetime, they're borrowed tools. I inherit and lose flecks
of each fingertip when I stroke a piano's note, greet a stranger,
sip from a mug. I shuffle and deal myself to unknowns
that might include ten thousand stones,
but I wonder about that first sacrifice when the everything gave itself up
to make us. If that's not evidence of God, it still proves
to me that each man is grander than a singularity,
and the world exists by a magic so large
that even as an accident I would call it divine, still some kind of love.

To the Kid Wearing a Che Guevara Belt Buckle at JFK Airport

I get it: the damn thing drives the hips
of the hip chicks wild back at high school.
With its slick-steel finish and macho beard
lined in chrome, your crotch appears daring,
wearing the jungle fighter as its pubic crown.
What you don't notice is when *Guerrillo Heroico*
holds up your pants, you're somebody

special as you unite a nation shredded
by its Revolution. Exiles burn like acetylene torches
when you advertise the man who selected their kin for death,
lined them up on the wall, and smoked a cigar as he watched them shot.
Back in Havana, the natives wait for your suburbs
to crumble in the aftermath of capitalism.
I should stop, step away righteous and glibly correct,

but who the hell am I?—barely half
the half-Cuban I claim as my heritage when I fill out forms
for the government or give an abridged lineage
to someone who catches my skin's slight tint.
Even my Spanish is in shambles, a weak tongue
parched, a muscle atrophied. I'd like to say
I lose twenty words a week, but that would imply I remember

a lot of names for things. In truth, I blanked
on the word for "check" last week in a Mexican restaurant.
I would never have tried it, too scared of drowning
in a conversation I couldn't control

and too ashamed to face native-speakers
who would patronize my attempt for a few extra bucks.
Am I that single-serving conquistador?

My grandparents died before I could meet them,
so the only Cuban I know is Dad who was born
"Armando Enrique" and grew up "Mandy."
These days, everyone calls him "Henry."
At five, he was one of the "Operation Peter Pan" kids
who left with one suitcase, and now he doesn't talk
about his homeland (maybe a quip about the pastoral)

unless it's to drool venom onto the names
of the people who stayed to pillage his birthright:
a family store and acres of cane.
Sometimes he tells the story of how Fidel's cronies visit
schoolkids and tell them to pray to God for ice cream.
It doesn't work. Then they're told to pray to Fidel.
Two scoops for everyone, at least this time.

When I was that age, I prayed no classmates
would call me a greasy Cuban, insisting
my surname was Spanish. Years later,
I realized I'd been right, since every Indian
was purged by European diseases or murdered, and I can't
claim I'm an African descendant of slaves: the only other option.
I'm European after all, same as my mother's "white" side of my family.

Spanish is just another way to be white,
sort of how ads have rebranded pork,
favorite flesh of my ancestors. In Cuba,
the explorers marched behind an infantry of snouts
that chewed rainforests to the roots. Oh, and Ernesto
Guevara wasn't Cuban either. He was another wealthy, white-faced
descendant of the Old World who decided what was best

for the little guy—first on that island, then, off to Africa
and the rest of his abridged world tour.
Kid, I know my real problem now. Seeing
that smug statement of El Che's face buckled
inches above your little soldier, I catch myself reflected
all too clearly and my insides tie themselves into a hangman's knot
that wrings the patience from my body.

Shawn Delgado earned a B.S. in Science, Technology, and Culture at the Georgia Institute of Technology, and his M.F.A. in Creative Writing from the University of North Carolina at Greensboro where he is currently teaching. He is the author of the chapbook A Sky Half-Dismantled, *and his poems have appeared or are forthcoming in* Connotations, The Cortland Review, Five Points, *and* Furious Season *among other places.*

Micheal O'Siadhail

Conversation with Shakespeare

The parsons, clowns, the porters, dukes and kings,
A sexton, jeweller, servant, witch or queen,
All playful, loving, tragic, lived mood swings
And battle fields our fantasy has seen.
Such wonders bred from such a fetid womb,
That plague-thronged London, city of disease,
A bloodstained hothouse where your plays will bloom
To entertain the hordes or even tease.
This cockpit holds *the vasty fields of France.*
Will Shakespeare you rehearse our human kind
Which in your wooden O you will entrance
And *eke out each performance with your mind.*
In heavens of our spirits' empty space
All breathe in your compassionate embrace.

I mix and match each burgeoned metaphor
And break the rule of unities, as rife
With words I let the highbrows I abhor
Confuse confusion with profusion's life.
I'll lift whatever line or theme I will –
Soliloques, asides, a quip, a pun,
Styles merged—Macbeth hires men to kill;—
His porter fuses tragedy with fun.
Let paradise and earth run parallel
This venal world a play within a play;
Inventing words I break convention's spell,
Speak what we feel, not what we ought to say,
Extravagance of heaven on the ground,
My rowdiness creation in the round.

A player rooted in the fetid Rose
Too busy to debauch, too wise or shrewd,
Exploiting ancient plots that you transpose
You're master of our every shifting mood.
Such rancour star-crossed lovers rise above
To bud before the summer's ripening breath,
Before ambition blots out heaven's love
And makes of Juliet a queen Macbeth.
Like Eves whose guilty flaw has eaten fruit
Your queens, who for their crowns have double-crossed
With falseness which should not find ground to root,
Must learn how hells are always heavens lost.
Some sell eternity to get a toy,
Your lovers know how joy delights in joy.

I weep the dust of all love's waking cries
And grieve myself to guess at others' smarts;
A rooted voice at once both wild and wise,
Am I the pardoned sum of all my parts?
Reality's a manifolded heart;
The forms of things unknown a poet's pen
Can move because he's moved himself.
I am all things to women as to men.
My role both Juliet's and Romeo's,
In my renaissance mind all opposites meet;
What's in a name? that which we call a rose
By any other name would smell as sweet.
Our life's kaleidoscope a paradise.
I never sign my name the same way twice.

Three Laments

(i)

How you and I so nearly never met.
Imagine if I'd missed that one small ad
Or hadn't looked and found that flat to let,
Which soon became our love life's launching pad.
The landlady's fire hung, she'd half said no;
'You wouldn't want a man to live above'—
She'd urged a lady in the flat below;
To think she nearly had bud-nipped our love!
Supposing you'd opposed this tenant man
And she'd refused to sign and do the deal,
I wouldn't have this lifelong gift you gave.
Where others had left off your love began;
Upon your arm, my bride, *you set my seal*
As firm as death and fiercer than this grave.

(ii)

For forty-four sweet years all thoughts were swapped.
Alone I'd list things in my mind to tell;
Will you now shape the tone I should adopt,
Your guessed response my ghosting sentinel?
I know you will and yet I wish for more,
I want to hear your words, your gentle tone
Caressing me with reasons as before;
I yearn for you anew in flesh and bone.
But everywhere your spirit's overspill—

I name you and once more you are so near;
Your presence wraps its care around me still,
As if your going leaves your love more here.
I must depend on wisdom you impart
In take-for-granted habits of my heart.

(iii)

O no, I'll never be an elegist
And you won't slip into my yesterday;
So I still say I kiss and not I kissed,
And keep to present tense *communiqués*.
I want no mourning or past tense laments,
I don't now shower you because you died
With rosy-coloured hindsight compliments—
God knows I'm proud I praised you on this side.
One lover and all things to this one man—
Such joy you'd kept incarnate and so fresh
Those almost forty-four sweet years we span.
We speak in spirit all we spoke in flesh.
The past and present hover in suspense;
We live our lives now in this double tense.

Micheal O'Siadhail's collections of poetry are The Leap Year *(1978),* Rungs of Time *(1980),* Belonging *(1982),* Springnight *(1983),* The Image Wheel *(1985),* The Chosen Garden *(1990),* Hail! Madam Jazz: New and Selected Poems *(Bloodaxe Books, 1992),* A Fragile City *(Bloodaxe Books, 1995),* Our Double Time *(Bloodaxe Books, 1998)* Poems 1975-1995 - Hail! Madam Jazz: New and Selected Poems *(Bloodaxe Books, 1999),* The Gossamer Wall *(Bloodaxe Books and Time Being Books 2002),* Love Life *(Bloodaxe Books 2005),* Globe *(Bloodaxe Books 2007) and* Tongues *(Bloodaxe Books 2010). His* Collected Poems *is due from Bloodaxe Books in September 2013.*

O'Siadhail has been a lecturer at Trinity College Dublin and a professor at the Dublin Institute for Advanced Studies. Among his many academic works are Learning Irish *(Yale University Press 1988) and* Modern Irish *(Cambridge University Press 1989). He was a member of the Arts Council of the Republic of Ireland (1988-93) and of the Advisory Committee on Cultural Relations (1989 -97), a founder member of Aosdána (Academy of distinguished Irish artists) and a former editor of* Poetry Ireland Review. *He was the founding chairman of* ILE *(Ireland Literature Exchange).*

Dionne Irving

How to Break an American Girl

The summer she was fifteen, men were the first lesson she learned about adulthood.

The Claudels were friends of her parents. Each of the Claudels was half French, but each one had it bred out with a strong set of ruddy Midwestern features. It made them look more like Idaho potato farmers with a name reeking of pretension. They spent the school year in America and then went to their home in Montpellier for July and August.

"What a wonderful experience it would be for you," Mrs. Claudel had said when she'd proposed the idea over dinner one night at her parents' house. Her mother made steaks, her idea of sophistication. She was trying to be a vegetarian that year, convincing herself that she didn't need meat. She poked at the steak over and over again without taking a bite, watching oily juices pool onto the electric orange Fiesta-ware her mother had picked out at Macy's the previous summer when she had hated her just a little bit less. She could feel her father's eyes on her, telling her to stop embarrassing them. And she thought, if she could, she would telegraph the message, "Fuck you."

She wanted to be anywhere. Anywhere but here at the dinner table with the adults. This was her mother's new thing, making her sit with everyone when they had dinner parties instead of letting her eat in her room like she used to.

Unlike the stab at vegetarianism (because just a month from that moment she returned to meat with nearly religious fervor), the affectation of bored teenager will follow her throughout life, making people call her self-centered, or boring, or both.

She only half listened to the way the Claudels talked about France. They nattered about how much she would learn and experience and about how quickly she would pick up French with the accompanying finger snap.

She thought of excuses she could make to get up to that bedroom and escape the tedium when Mrs. Claudel grabbed her arm.

"And of course, I need the help, too."

And she did. She had three children, all under the age of six.

In this particular story, Mrs. Claudel will be the cuckold.

Her parents agreed more easily than they should have. But they were those kinds of parents. Dumb about all the wrong things. They had rules when it came to curfews (11:30) and alcohol (never), all the while letting her wear tiny skirts that drew the kind of gaze they were afraid of.

They had rules when it came to curfews (11:30) and alcohol (never), all the while letting her wear tiny skirts that drew the kind of gaze they were afraid of.

And so she went. She went alone with a kind of bravado that startled even her. She imagined she would be a different person in Europe that the travel would be her chrysalis, and on the other side of the world she would emerge a new person.

She drank wine for the first time on the plane overseas, flirted with a British boy with pretty blue eyes and no chin, and finally got the train from London to Paris. "Who was that girl" she imagined people thinking, dazzled by her American glamour. She was Jackie O. She was Grace Kelly.

And then she was there, the train from Paris depositing her in Montpelier's city center, in its overly cramped train station. Outside waiting for her in front of a tiny car, dusty underneath the blazing hot sun was Mr. Claudel. She had never seen him like this before, his shirt bright pink, printed with tiny white goldfish, and unbuttoned midway down his chest.

These were his lady-snatching threads.

"And so you've arrived darling!"

He clapped his hands together and reached out to hug her, which felt awkward and weird, both because her family were not hugging people and because she had never so much as shaken his hand. The darling affectation was even weirder than the hug. He called her darling as they drove up into the hills, once even sliding his hand over the back of her head, down her shoulders, ever so slightly brushing her shoulders.

The Claudels' house was a 200-year-old cottage, situated on a bluff above the city center. The dusty gardens, the moldering old barn, the cistern, and the clean, slightly salty air made her love it all the more. It was everything she had imagined France to be.

Her skin went from bronzed to dark in a matter of days. She took to lining her eyes in a deep kohl as she would continue to do for the rest of her life, and during her second week there, without telling anyone, she went into a French barber and had her hair cut very short, just like Jean Seberg in *Breathless*.

The Claudels made her feel like an adult even though she wasn't. They left her alone during the days with the children; three curly-haired children with what she decided were overly American names (Jennifer, Joshua and Jack). Mr. Claudel worked in an office over an hour away and some days Mrs. Claudel worked at the small bookshop that they owned in the city center and on others she shopped or had lunch with friends. She liked her time alone with the children. She sang to them and was a willing assistant in construction of mud pies or tree forts.

Mrs. Claudel taught her to drive one Saturday and she picked it up quickly, learning to maneuver the Renault up and down the hills, stalling only three or four times.

"It will be better this way," Mrs. Claudel said. "This way you won't be stuck on this hill all day and you can run errands for me."

In the evening, even if she was worn out, she ventured down from the hills. At night after the children had gone to bed she would walk the thirty minutes to the city center, up and down dark alleyways,

...a pack of girls called out to her one night and she'd approached the group nearly a foot shorter than she was with stick straight hair and blood red nails.

"You are American?"

"Yes."

and past the cinema that showed mainly American films. She'd never made friends easily, but a pack of girls called out to her one night and she'd approached the group nearly a foot shorter than she was with stick straight hair and blood red nails.

"You are American?"

"Yes."

They'd gathered around her, peppering her questions. They loved her hair, wanted to talk about Michael Jordan, and Michael Jackson. They told her stories in English and she did her best with her French. They mixed up idioms and she over explained. They were mostly her age, but everything about them seemed older, better, classier. They smoked Gauloise, wore scarves, and seemed to dress almost entirely in slim black pants and pretty print dresses. They introduced her to friends and friends of friends, who had parties, who smoked hashish who drank wine from gallon sized jugs that they would sip instead of slugging the way boys did at parties back home.

So off she went. She took the children to the shore, to Sete and to Aubais and St Gilles and anywhere that she could before their parents got them home.

She will think this is the France of Baldwin, Bardot and Baker. She will think France will save her instead of ruin her.

At a party, midway through the summer, someone, she won't be sure who, will put a glass in her hand and the room will get hotter, and the party will swell as more and more people will crowd into the living room and into the cramped kitchen. Everyone will finally get drunk enough, high enough, and someone will turn the volume up again and she will feel it pounding between her temples. It will have a strange melody, will not be danceable, will be grating. But there was something soothing in its consistency.

The boys looked at her strangely, as though they were unsure they knew her, or unsure they were seeing her in the right place. The girls didn't even acknowledge her presence.

She wandered into the backyard, feeling hot and stuffy. The conversations were rapid and quick, the daytime patience of the friends exhausted. Lulled by alcohol and desire, she talked to anyone who looked at her.

This will lead her in her adult life to drink too much at parties, to drink until she forgets.

She gulped the wine, both for something to do and because she didn't know any better.

She was a slip of a girl, really, long and thin in the way girls are at fifteen, and then, never again. She will spend the rest of her life deep in pills and diets and starvation trying to get back to that point.

In memories it will be much more romantic, but in truth a tall boy with a faint mustache and a pork pie hat just kind of grabbed at her, whispered to her in French that she was beautiful, making something tingle inside that made her feel excited and powerful. He said something to her she didn't understand, frowning at her, but the darkness covered the parts of his face that would help her understand if he was sad or angry. He put his hands around her waist, moved with her to the music, "Move your hips," he whispered into her ear over and over again.

She did the best she could, struggled to find the way she should move to the syncopated beats and eventually just gave up and shook her ass, her cheeks hot with embarrassment.

"Oh yes," he murmured, twirling her. "You've got it now."

Eventually he pulled her into a corner, rolled a joint and shared it with her. Kissed her so hard, mashed his mouth so forcefully into hers that she tasted blood. It was an eventful four hours.

Eventually he pulled her into a corner, rolled a joint and shared it with her. Kissed her so hard, mashed his mouth so forcefully into hers that she tasted blood.

It was an eventful four hours.

They are hours she will try to capture again and again with drugs, and sex, and vacations, and shopping.

Just before dawn he took her into the smokehouse at the edge of the

"You scared?" he said, in a way that she thought he must have thought sounded tender.

She shook her head no...

property. The place worked as a small farm and hung up where she could see were the shady outlines of pigs and chickens. The sawdust shifted under their feet and the boy drew her in close.

"You scared?" he said, in a way that she thought he must have thought sounded tender.

She shook her head no, even though she was terrified and excited. The boy stuck his hand under her shirt, his tongue in her mouth and, to her surprise, all she felt was boredom.

This feeling too is one she will run from as an adult: constant, crushing boredom. Conquest is never as sweet as the chase.

She kissed him back harder, trying to figure out what was wrong. They stayed there for a while, until she begged off, tipsy and dizzy and a little nauseated. Back to the Renault and down the winding hills as the sun came up a little at a time, illuminating first the red dust on the road and then the walled fortress of the town itself and finally, as she sputtered toward the long pebbled drive of the Claudels' home, the ocean itself.

The next day she took a long walk with the children, and chased them around the overgrown gardens. Mrs. Claudel took them all into town to buy a raft of pastries and cheese, of jams in tiny pots and cured meats. She picked up half a dozen jars of cornichons and four pounds of butter before they all piled back into the Renault and made their way up the hillside. That evening the Claudels had friends in town from Paris. She was instructed to feed the children early and she put them into bed before the sunset. Mrs. Claudel was not one to indulge in the type of French mothering that would ruin a dinner party.

The guests arrived in cars loaded with four, then two, then six people. She greeted them at the door, collected an assortment of scarves and handbags that she tucked inside the pantry door. They hugged her, they called her "la petit negress charmant," and one man, a business associate of Mr. Claudel whom she'd met a time or two, grabbed her ass and then he gave her a big wet kiss on her cheek.

She wasn't invited to the table either and she ate dinner alone in her room, reading, but listening too, for the burst of laughter, the clink of glasses or footsteps on the stairs.

She fell asleep eventually and when she woke up it was still dark, and she heard the crunch of cars on the gravel driveway and the last goodbyes and she realized slowly that it wasn't yet morning. She went downstairs to the kitchen now empty. The sink piled high with pots and pans and the counter a mess of sticky wine glasses and plates with leftover pools of sauce and congealed flecks of butter. She would have to wash these in the morning. There was still a smattering of voices from outside. She opened one of the pots, barely chewing before she swallowed the remnants of a cassoulet. The duck grease made her mouth slick and she wiped at it with the back of her hand.

She poured herself wine into one of the children's juice glasses. Out in the garden she stood behind a shrub and she watched the last of the adults migrate into the house for one last drink, one last cigarette before getting on the road. She was still learning to smoke and took tentative puffs from the hand-rolled cigarette one of the party guests had given her and sipped the wine, looking up into a sky so clear and bright, nothing like the sky she knew at home. She wrote, during this time, in her journal. She had wanted then to be a writer, and before that an actress, and later on, a psychiatrist.

One day she wouldn't remember wanting to have been anything at all.

"You look," he said, "like a garden nymph standing here surrounded by beauty."

It was Mr. Claudel. He startled her and she dribbled a little wine down the front of the pink peasant blouse she'd purchased that afternoon while wandering through the alleyways of the city as she waited for Mrs. Claudel to finish shopping.

He sat in the garden chair next to her and stared at the night sky.

"I never get used to the sky in America, with all the lights ruining the stars," he said.

Below them, Montpelier glittered with its few nighttime lights and she could see the outline of the old Roman aqueducts surrounding the town, holding it in from the rest of the world. She thought then it was like a fairytale, like a castle with a moat.

Later those aqueducts would seem more like boundaries, far less romantic, a way to keep some in and others out.

"You see the aqueducts, yes?" he said.
"Yes," she said. "But I thought those kinds of things were only in Italy."
"The Romans," he said, "were everywhere."
She tried to imagine it. Roman soldiers with spears and shields marching through southern France but she kept picturing the mustachioed French kid dressed like a gladiator.
"The Romans were an epic civilization."
When he said the word "Romans" with his accent, it sounded like "Ramens" and she had to keep herself from laughing.
"Are they very old?" she asked instead.

Like she didn't know. Seduction without knowing it.

"I believe they were built around 19BC."

Like he knew. Like the others in Montpelier, he told lies about the city as easily as he told them about himself. They were really built in the 17th century.

He took rolling paper and tobacco from his pocket. He rolled her a fresh cigarette and then one for himself.
"It's amazing that they're still here," she said
"Beauty never fades entirely. It may be diminished, but it won't go away. The Romans knew how to make things that were both beautiful and functional."
She liked the way he spoke, the way he tossed things like this out offhand. He lit both cigarettes and handed her one.
"Are you having a nice summer?" he asked her.
"Very nice," she said. "And educational."
It was something her parents had trained her to say, and Mr. Claudel

laughed.

"It shouldn't be educational. You are young, and you need to have fun."

This idea of fun, in its very French way, would be the excuse he used for everything that happened from then on. When he spirited her away to the beach, took her to a wonderful restaurant, bought expensive dresses she would never wear again, and when he finally came to her bed.

"I guess," she said.

She took a drag of the cigarette and accidentally inhaled, the smoke stinging her throat and making her eyes water. She coughed hard and Mr. Claudel came over from his chair and smacked her on the back.

"Be careful," he said. "And don't let your parents know that we let you smoke. Or drink, for that matter. "

He sat next to her on the grass instead of going back to the other chair. It felt nice to have him at her feet, to sit above him.

"I'm so glad you could come. Every young girl should have the chance to go abroad. And Martine really needed the help this summer."

He got quiet again and she tried to think of something to say, something to talk about that made her sound grownup.

"I've really liked all the walking and the shopping here. I feel like I've lost a ton of weight just walking to the market and back."

It got so quiet and she could hear the chirp of cicadas in the trees.

"Did you know," he said finally, "that you can exercise your abdomen just by holding your breath?"

"That can't be true."

"Oh yes," he said getting very animated. "I've read all about it. They've done these tests at an American University, where they show that holding your breath if done correctly, can actually strengthen the abdominal wall. Make it stronger. Let's hold our breath for a moment. Let's see if we can feel it."

They were quiet for a minute, until finally she exhaled in a dramatic puff and Mr. Claudel smiled and exhaled slowly.

"Did you feel it," he asked.

"Kind of," she said. Mostly her lungs and her cheeks burned, because really, she'd wanted to best him.

"You must not be doing it correctly."

He got up and came around behind her and put his hand on her abdomen.

"Hold your breath," he said.

She sucked in and she felt the warm, hot, pressure of his hand on her stomach.

"Hold it as long as you can."

She felt the tightening of her stomach muscles and the pressure of his hand became more firm. She could feel the muscles in her stomach flex and tighten, and she heard Mr. Claudel's breathing quicken.

Don't you see she knew what she was doing?

"Okay," he said. "Breathe out."

She exhaled in a rush just as Mrs. Claudel came out into the yard, and Mr. Claudel straightened up suddenly, putting his hands on his hips

"Did you feel the difference," he asked curtly.

"Yes," she said. "I did."

> She felt the tightening of her stomach muscles and the pressure of his hand became more firm. She could feel the muscles in her stomach flex and tighten, and she heard Mr. Claudel's breathing quicken.

See, the reader hates her already, has imagined that she is the kind of Lolita that comes in under the pretense of childcare and seduces married men. And maybe she did. But maybe she didn't. There is a way that those who are beautiful fall into these moments, happen into them, as though they have no control.

In her thirties she picks a simple man—simple looking, simple speaking, mayonnaise on Wonder Bread. He is the kind of person so flat that the main draw will be his paycheck. She knows she is beautiful. He is dazzled. Her features have that sharpness, like cut glass. There is none of the softness that makes some women cute, but the kind of steel beauty that feels frightening.

She talks about marriage to her co-workers after their third date. She starts looking at cushion-cut rings six months in and reads *Modern Bride* in secret during their first year living together, hiding the magazine under the bed or in the linen closet. And there are ideas about a wedding in Newport and summers on Cape Cod.

"Oh yes," she hears herself saying one night over cocktails. "I love fly fishing." Just like Mr. Claudel, she learns the way that lies seem to slip out of her so easily. A love for dogs, tow-headed children, asparagus. She starts growing out her hair, and when she speaks to her sorority sisters in Boston on a weekend trip away from Rhode Island, it is in the future perfect. "My future husband." Wink wink, nudge nudge. "This is where we'll buy." "This is how we'll decorate." The future perfect is more interesting than the present complicated.

She gets bored of him, like you knew she would.

She starts to hate him. And toward the end, she spends a lot of time waiting for him, listening to excuses for missed dinners or movies. She starts to spend entire nights away from the house. She meets a new set of girlfriends and stays out until 4 am, 5am, 6 and 7 even. But he isn't fazed. Takes it all in stride, says he is glad she is having fun.

She does things then that would shock you. That would disgust him and she feels nothing.

"This is the American idea of fun." This is what Mr. Claudel said to her when he would email her in college and in her twenties. It was the same thing he would text her when he met one of her boyfriends at her parents' house or saw pictures from a trip to Mexico with her girlfriends. It was this phrase more than anything that made her feel ashamed.

Man can't live by beauty alone. So one evening she sits on the stoop recovering from a hangover, enjoying the early evening breeze on her face. The little girl from next door walks over and plops herself down next to her with a kind of world-weariness.

She's met the little girl once before. She can't remember if her name is Karen or Kristin.

"Have you seen Brian?" the little girl says by way of greeting.

"I don't know who Brian is," she answers. She checks her watch again.

He is over an hour late. She thinks about leaving and wonders if he would notice.

The little girl looks at her pityingly. She is cute in the way ugly children sometimes are, her features a little too large for her tiny head. She will be a striking woman when she gets older.

"Can I come in?" the little girl asks. "I want to see if your house looks any different than ours."

It is nearly winter and the last of the late afternoon sun dips in the sky as she considers what it means to be the childless couple who let small children into their condo after dark. What type of person does that? she thinks.

"Okay," she says. "But just for a second."

By the time they get inside it is already dark. With no lights on, the condo feels colder than normal. The fluorescent lights reflect off the newly purchased stainless steel appliances, the granite countertops they haven't used for anything other than to do lines of coke, and she thinks again about why she let the little girl in the house. She doesn't know what she is doing.

"Don't you have any toys?" the girl asks.

"No."

The little girl walks all around the apartment. She opens cabinets and drawers and she just lets her. She sits on the couch in the living room while the girl looks under beds, in closets, pulls things out and examines them. The girl finally comes into the living room and sits next to her on the couch.

"You really don't have any toys," she says with a sigh.

It's after seven now, and she still hasn't heard from him. She doesn't know yet that this will be it, that after this night, things will be over between them.

Yes, he was cheating, with the kind of girl who owns more than one pair of sweatpants, who gets her hair cut in a shopping mall. She will find digital pictures of the woman in various states of polyester-undress. Cheap and tawdry, she will finally feel something.

"Do you have any cookies at least?"

"No."

There isn't any food in the house at all. Nothing to eat, nothing to cook with, lots of paper plates and takeout menus but that is all. She wants, all of a sudden, to get the little girl out of the house so she can pull apart his closet like she's done so many nights before, searching for a note, a receipt, something she hasn't even thought of yet.

The little girl sighs.

"You don't have anything good."

It isn't pretty, but men love hysterical beauty and he begs her to stay.

She doesn't do cuckold well. She doesn't have presence of mind to do what Mrs. Claudel did, which was to face it, to pack her things, to send her home.

When he gets home things will be broken. When he gets home she will be screaming. When he gets home she will be broken. Not by him, but in spite of him. It isn't pretty, but men love hysterical beauty and he begs her to stay.

Dionne Irving's work has appeared in The Missouri Review, The Crab Orchard Review, The New Delta Review *and other places. She is currently at work on a historical novel called* Quint. *Dionne is a professor at St. Mary's College, a women's college in Notre Dame, Indiana.*

Tim Payne

On Reassembling the Cover to *Memory's Handgrenade*: An Apology

I cut up your book. A gift
from a friend, for watching him marry
a woman I barely knew, a knife
given to me as collateral
helped, all told, in its way.

If it's any consolation, I sweated
that rented tux with its heft
in pocket, handle engraved
by some girl at a food court kiosk,

intercom rattling above, fretful
for lights left on, asking for someone
to claim their kids. She didn't know
she was working an end to your book,
couldn't anticipate its *Plasti-Kleer Fold-On Adjustable Jacket*
any more than I.

What is it about disaster that craves
so many syllables? Something more than eloquence
flash-fried the bodies at Pompeii. Their fingers
weren't gnawed to rock
by historiography. I know my friend

didn't want this,
thought the script would wind
around the blade like kudzu taking back a house,

thought the girl, polite, never touching
on the point of these knives,

would limit them to one life. Don't you see,

now, to read these letters,
I'd have to skin the thing
that brought them to me, carve
out a difference between ash
on the wind and nostalgia?

At Earthset

Writing you just now,
I wanted to say many things
have been said
about the moon,

but little standing upon its surface.
And the sky hangs like a black sheet
that never dirties
and never wheels away.

No voices from the ground,
my co-pilot's face still
angled toward stars we were sent
to ignore. Can you imagine

what he sees
in that concave mirror, your eyes
would do as you fell
into inner vacuums,

the quiet,
the limbs, the mind
rebounding against itself, its need
to learn by weighted opposites,

the disappointment, to hang forever
in dark, palimpsest of a mouth,
like a doorway flanked by mirrors,
to sag into not-knowing?
There is nothing at all here
that can harm us.

Father and Son

Out past the castaway skeletons
of train tracks and chicken farms,
my father and I cut through the drifts

looking for a gut to puddle
in its own warmth, clumsy bag
to break apart with a hiss of metal

on velvet. I see a cherry snow cone
blooming between haunches,
children somewhere laughing.

Imagine the surprise, buckshot,
aptly named, bounding through abdomen
like seeking cover in the understory,

picking through the brush and clearings
of an innermost, soon-to-be
non-being, some undisclosed corner of God.

A knife click taunts the stillness.
My father tells me to do it here.
Field Dressing, like we could stretch

for miles, grow large enough
to bind these woods with our bodies.
Build into me a calm heat.

So far from town, and so cold,
tired knuckles of frost shake
from that stiffness with every thrust,

the blade and the wet splayed open
along rocks with no eyes to close
or witness what we ruin for each other.

Tim Payne recently graduated from the Master's Program at the University of West Georgia. He hasn't won much of anything or appeared many other places. This is, in fact, his only publication; but he hopes to change that shortly.

Bruce McEver

Year of the Rooster

I

In Bali, a chorus of roosters conspire
to raise the sun and divine
each morning of the world.
A golden hue lumens the palm tangle
edging terraced rice patties,
stacked like pancakes and soggy
from an irrigation system
shared since antiquity.

I visit the Ubud market,
that smells of incense and spices,
and jumbled with women selling saffron sarongs
and scarves, to buy a canang,
a small palm-leaf tray
of offering flowers.

I make a path through the hawkers
of batik and sandalwood carvers
to a forest at the end of town.
Drawn by the sound of water spewing
from a crevice in the ground
I wander down mossy stairs.

Over the cascade, arches a bridge
whose rails are stone serpents.
They crawl through a square portal
cut in the airy root veil

of a banyan tree spanning
the holy stream.

Beyond this portal, stands a stone sanctuary
where I bathe with other worshippers
in a clear pool fountain-headed by marbled dragons
to wash away my travel husk
and demons and pray.

I dry and wrap the requisite sarong
and tie a sash around me to cross
the temple threshold opening us
to the sky like a plea.
Barefoot, I enter the inner temple yard
scattered with altars wrapped
in black-checked and bright-yellow cloths.

II

The priest, white turbaned
and robed, rings a bell
to punctuate incantations.
I sit cross-legged to address the presence
in the prescribed manner.
I cleanse my hands in the smoking ember
of my incense stick next to my canang
and clasp the proper flower
to my forehead before tossing it away.

White first, for the Great One,
then amber and mauve
for lesser and local gods.
I am careful not to offend anyone,
under the gaze of fierce
stone temple guardians.
Irreverent monkeys play
over the inner sanctum.
I soon come into the silence

and find a presence all around,
in each empty stone seat,
high on the pagoda platforms,
silhouetted by the far volcano,
that invites the mystery—
no—becomes the mystery
those roosters scare up
each morning.

Celebrating the Moon Festival
At the Pingyao International
Financiers' Club

Why does the moon tend to be full
when people are apart?
　　　　　—Su Dong Po, 1076

Over its bar, the Club shows global pretentions:
four clocks tracking time in London,
Moscow, Beijing, and New York,
yet no one speaks Russian anymore,
and barely enough English to manage a red wine.

But here, during the Qing dynasty, the first financiers
gave up their prosperous dye works
after discovering paper
could carry the same value as silver.
They got other merchants to leave deposits
in their vaults who, in turn, traveled
lighter and safer without bodyguards.
Setting out on shaggy horses along ten foot thick walls
that still surround this city,
their clients carried coded paper
they'd later exchange for coins
at other Rishengchang branches
when they got to Peking,
Nanking, or Chang'an.

And just last night, I strolled those streets
the first bankers left long ago,

past their courtyards of carved screens
and intrigue, protected from plundering Huns
behind the huge walls and watch towers
like a dragon guarding its hoard,
unable to contain an idea that has since
spilled through the earth.

Bruce McEver is the Chairman of Berkshire Capital in New York City and lives in Salisbury, Connecticut on Utopia Farm with his wife Christina. His work has appeared in Ploughshares, The Cortland Review, The Atlanta Review, *and others. His first full-length collection* Split Horizon *was published by Jeanne Duval Editions. He is a founding supporter of* Poetry@TECH *in Atlanta and on the board of* Poet's House *in New York.*

Anne Marie Macari

Cave River

Alone, I left the visible world.
How hard my eyes pressed

but still no sight. Some things

abhor light and I almost
understand them growing

in their slime. I stayed
in darkness, stayed till

the winding sheet began to come

undone around me, all of me
loosening, separating, even

the pieces of my own spine
unhooked, and bits of me

floating off with the river—arm

ear   teeth—the cave a throat
swallowing me. Later, it spit me up,

carried me out like a boat—

my body returning to me—light
that picked my pieces up

and made of me
what it could.

Horse

Candamo Cave, Spain

High up the wall you seemed to move
in the fatty lamplight—
your short legs and erect mane

and in the grasslands a sea of you
How you fell
How you tasted

Tell me the story of when first
I held you femur to flank
miles we raced one body

the wind splayed around us How
you let me ride any direction
Lips pulled back snorting

How you wore me clinging
my legs raw   the marriage
long and lonely   Runaway

Anne Marie Macari is the author of four books of poetry, including Red Deer, *forthcoming from Persea, and* She Heads Into the Wilderness *(Autumn House, 2008). In 2000 Macari won the APR/ Honickman first book prize for* Ivory Cradle, *which was followed by* Gloryland *(2005, Alice James Books). She has also coedited, with Carey Salerno,* Lit From Inside: 40 Years of Poetry From Alice James Books. *She teaches in the Drew University MFA Program in Poetry & Poetry in Translation.*

Rupert Fike

Motel Room Notes

It's six in the morning, and through the wall
I can hear someone taking a shower.
Day has begun. There's a plane to catch,
or maybe there's a lover still in bed
wanting more, basking in their scent,
miffed at the other for washing it off.
Always someone up before us, always,
the worm never safe from them
same as we're never safe from the old saws
prefaced by, *Well, you know what they say.*
Yes. We do know what they say.
We've heard it from maiden aunts, winos,
change-jingling gents old before their time.
Not that we haven't done it ourselves,
traded threadbare homilies with strangers .

But isn't it the quarrelsome among us
who poke, keep the big campfire going?
Like Rabbis parsing Midrash passages
deep into a Brooklyn night, or Gershwin's
caution, *It ain't necessarily so.*
Or like that Glasgow bookstore clerk,
just me and him with such weather outside
his radio announced it, *Cyclonic.*
This I took as my cue to offer,
"Well, we take what we get."
(the Yank accent not helping).
"Of course we take what we get!" he snapped.
But seeing I wanted to buy a book,

he softened, "Ah, Scots, we're a phlegmatic lot."
Here was his peace offering, best he could do.
I debated seeing his *phlegmatic*
and raising him a *lachrymose*
regarding my storm-marred holiday,
but no, better to just part with a "Cheers,"
and retreat to my once-grand hotel,
its lobby filled with Danes tapping laptops,
their backpacks on the floor like tired dogs.
Yet still the place held a whiff of intrigue,
so unlike this prefab room and thin walls
where next door the shower's just ended,
and I can again hear the Interstate,
its ceaseless hum, its lanes already filled,
everybody out there with a head start.

Rupert Fike's collection, Lotus Buffet *(Brick Road Poetry Press) was named Finalist in the 2011 Georgia Author of the Year Awards. He has been nominated for Pushcart prizes in fiction and poetry with work appearing in* The Southern Review of Poetry, Rosebud, Natural Bridge, The Georgetown Review *and others. He has a poem inscribed in a downtown Atlanta plaza, and his non-fiction book,* Voices from the Farm, *is now in its second printing with accounts of life in a spiritual community in the 1970s.*

Mark Benedict

Baby, the Rain Must Fall

Billy was darkening. His History teacher, Mr. Hooper, was yucking it up to the class about Billy's crumpled homework. Hooper razzed him about one thing or another on an almost daily basis. But always in the crispest tone, the fanciest language. Dude wasn't British but had a British kind of thing going on. In response Billy usually looked away and let the dark feeling shelter and obscure him like a cloak. Today, though, he felt hyper-present; the darkness was there but it was inside him instead of over him, and it stirred him up instead of calming him down. Hooper had finally moved on to the day's lesson, but not Billy. He rubbed his closed fist into the desktop, sad, simmering. How could this chump-lick think he'd just sit back and take it? Billy could have him begging for mercy in thirty seconds, and felt the pull of the idea. It was amazing, really, how easily you could unloose the invisible ropes of restraint and do something really psycho.

He decided to unloose them. He got up from his desk and walked slowly to Hooper at the blackboard. Hooper's eyes registered surprise but as Billy got closer Hooper's eyes got bigger and fear entered them. Billy raised his fist aloft saying how ya like me now bitch, thinking that maybe he'd just harass him for a few minutes, but Hooper instantly cowered and begged Billy not to hit him. This Billy could not stomach; he actually felt a surge of nausea. He let it rip: three to the face to start, real crunchers, followed by jabs to the stomach. Hooper doubled over; blood from his nose dripped to the floor. From behind, Billy heard the other students gasping. He wondered at how closely it resembled cheering. And the violence felt beautiful, like he was becoming more of a man with each blow. Shrieking like a girl, Hooper stumbled over to the corner. Billy practically laughed. Retard was actually cornering himself.

When school security finally arrived to drag Billy away, he looked down into the Hooper slump and tried to make eye contact. But Hooper kept ducking his head to avoid it. Then Billy hawked up some phlegm and spat into Hooper's face, a total slimer, and told him to have his wife give Billy a call if she wanted to get laid for a change.

Oh, man. What an exit. If he had planned it for weeks he couldn't have done it better. He was so psyched he hardly minded these two goons digging their fingers into his arms as they shoved him toward the principal's office.

Seven years later, eating peanuts and drinking beer in a dark bar, Billy was thinking over the past and realized with some amusement that the time with Hooper had launched his career as a hoodlum. Not that he was actually criminal, but all through his travels, through trade school and even in his work as a furniture maker, people always somehow kept their distance. He traced hearts on the side of his frosty beer mug. On his right, his friend Rocco was sucking on a brew and cheering on the Yankees game on the TV. It was like the thing with Hooper had given him a permanent shine somehow, a kind of outlaw luster. People knew not to fuck with him.

And the aftermath hadn't been nearly as bad as Billy would've thought. Hooper was more respected than loved, and when you got right down to it, he wasn't all that respected, either. So no one's heart was broken. And Hooper wasn't broken too bad, either: his nose was, and his ribs, but it was far from the most brutal beat-down ever. Billy got sent to a juvenile delinquent facility for a month, and there was a brief trial, but whatever. When he returned to school, in late spring of his sophomore year, most people avoided him, but it was different from the way they avoided him before. Before it was like they didn't quite see him, whereas now they saw him and tried to act like they didn't. Billy didn't mind this. It was like having friends somehow. Only better, because you didn't actually have to talk to anyone. Nah, he didn't mind at all. He started working out. Bought a black leather jacket at the thrift store.

Billy watched absently as the couple to his left whispered and smiled at each other. No, he wasn't a criminal, not yet, but there was rage in him. His body flamed with anger all the time. But what was he so angry about? It was hard to say. Maybe just all the pointless noise in the world, all the damn chit-chatty people. That was the good thing about Rocco: dude kept a tight lip. What, after all, was the good of talking?

Women, though. You had to talk to them or else you'd never get any. He personally hadn't gotten any in three years, and it wasn't a record he wanted to extend.

Billy considered this couple. Guy had a kind of cheetah face, no great shakes, but he was dressed in a crisp white shirt and tan suit coat, and it was obvious somehow that he did okay with the ladies. This particular lady, a brunette in a white top and grey miniskirt, laughed loudly after nearly everything the guy said. It was obvious that they were not in a relationship, just as it was obvious that he would sleep with her tonight, and maybe again next week, and still never ever call her girlfriend. But the other couple in the bar, seated in a booth, was another story. The girl was blonde and re-laxed, but the guy had an anxious, insincere glint in his eye: he was keeping secrets, telling her what she wanted to hear. And this was more consistent with the stories Billy overheard at the furniture factory. Unless you were like the well-dressed guy, a born charm cheetah, you had your work cut out for you. It was a sad thing, a mean thing, but it seemed for guys like Billy love would always have to be tricked out of women, stolen.

He resolved to start tricking them. The next day he set up a profile on an online dating site using made-up details about himself. After a month, he had gotten it on with three different chicks. Lawyers, as Billy had suspected, did pretty well. Or did they? None of these chicks were particularly good-looking and some, like this Alice lady, who wore ghoulish eye make-up and tattered muskratty furs, were older and verged on ugly. He wanted young beauties. With help from a computer programmer friend of Rocco's, Billy set up a website for a fake model-recruitment business. Then he set up a photography studio in his apartment. This brought in the beauties all right, but after six months only three of them had given themselves to him. One of them, Cindy, was a piping hot brunette, and almost made the whole operation worthwhile, but it was a one-time thing and left him sick with lust.

Son of a bitch. What did a guy have to do to get some love?

The porn movie was Rocco's idea. It was originally going to be fake, just like the photo shoots, but Billy figured that it wouldn't be that much more work to do the damn thing. You could do a lot on the computer these days. Or Rocco's friend Sam could, anyway. And maybe there'd be some way to sell it. Rocco wrote the script, Billy auditioned the women. At last: hot chicks who were more than willing to do it. In fact, they had to do it with him up front; doing it with him was the audition. It was a gloriously long audition process. It was all he'd ever wanted in life: for his manhood to be sore from actual fucking rather than from pretend fucking. Finally, he selected three beauties and filming began. He starred and directed, while Rocco did the lights and played a small role. Sam edited and saw to other technical matters.

Six months later, the film was complete and had been sold for six figures. Billy kept half for himself, planning to pay bonuses to the girls out of that, and split the other between Rocco and Sam. This seemed, to Billy, more than fair. Rosalyn, the star of the film and his live-in girlfriend, didn't seem to agree but oh well. Sweet Rosalyn, with her butterscotch hair and meowing face. At a dinner meeting to discuss their next project, a soft-core porn with a bigger crew, Rocco and Sam glowered in the booth like bullied orphans. They were still disgruntled about their pay for the last film. Billy once again explained that his extra pay was justified: the director was the man, man. Sam replied that they had gone into it as three equal partners. Billy shook his head once, to signify that no they hadn't, and again, to signify that the conversation was over. More likely, anyway, they were just jealous that they hadn't come away with a meow-faced beauty. Amateurs. Ingrates. Still, to show some goodwill, he sent them each a check for an extra grand the following week. But when production on the new project started, at a small soundstage at the outskirts of town, Rocco and Sam didn't show.

What the shit. What the fuck. Billy didn't have time for this, and deserved better. And when Rocco finally returned Billy's voicemails, his tone had no love, no respect. He simply said he and Sam had decided they wouldn't be working on the project. When Billy hung up the phone, he spun around to face the set wall and punched a hole in it. It didn't help his mood that

Rosalyn was gone this week, away shooting her own movie.

He was sad but not surprised when he learned that Rocco and Sam planned to kill him. There had been signs, after all: hang-ups from unknown numbers, Rocco's car following close behind when he looked in his rearview. And then a crew member told him that Rocco had contacted a number of them, trying to get information about Billy's schedule. It was a sad day: dude was his oldest friend. It was hard to believe and yet he knew it was true. They were going to kill him. They were really going to kill him.

But not if Billy killed them first. The sorrow passed, replaced with the old sizzling anger. He arranged to get his hands on a pistol. Rocco was easy to find: the bar. Billy hunched down behind Rocco's car, waiting. When Rocco came out of the bar, Billy blasted him twice: once in the stomach, a real gut-buster, and once in his stupid face. Rocco sputtered around, groaning like a gramps, then collapsed. Billy learned that Sam, hip to Rocco's fate, had shacked up with a woman at a motel and was making plans to leave town. Billy blasted through the door. Rosalyn, as he had figured, was the woman. She and Sam were half-dressed and seated at a table drinking beer and playing cards. They leapt up, shrieking, begging. Then they were on the floor, dead and oozing all over.

Driving back to the set, Billy thought, randomly, of the day he got his leather jacket. The girl at the counter, a smoochy-lipped brunette wearing an old-timey polka-dot dress, eyed him the whole time he was there, checking him out, maybe, or else just making sure he didn't steal anything. But either possibility seemed pretty good. The thrift store, like high school, like everywhere at that time, seemed like a respectful place.

He parked at the soundstage lot and walked quickly toward the entrance. It had turned out to be a meaner world than he'd like, crueler, harder-biting, but he didn't make it. Anyhow, he hadn't talked to his mom in years. He should really call her.

Mark Benedict recently completed an MFA in Fiction Writing at Sarah Lawrence College. He has previously published in The Abecedary Project *and* Mad Swirl.

CPSIA information can be obtained at www.ICGtesting.com
Printed in the USA
LVOW01s1035210913

353510LV00001B/1/P